Mastery o

Power, Success

Frank C. Haddock

Alpha Editions

This edition published in 2022

ISBN : 9789356902053

Design and Setting By
Alpha Editions
www.alphaedis.com
Email - info@alphaedis.com

PART 21

POWER FOR SUCCESS

WHAT THIS BOOK TEACHES

This book brings to a close that portion of MASTERY OF SELF, which deals with the art of Success-Magnetism.

Acquiring magnetism is a constructive effort. It is a building process. You are rearing a structure. You rise, from the foundation, through successive stories to the culminating peak. The most pleasing, notable structures men build from granite and steel and wood, tower like a Woolworth Building or a Rheims Cathedral—higher and higher, until they finally reach a gold- tipped crown or spire, high in the sunlit sky.

And so, in rearing your invisible shrine of personal Success- magnetism, we now come to the topmost peak of the structure. This book gives you the crowning inspirations, tipped and topped with the final "Golden Laws of Magnetism in all Applied Life."

Master these lessons in the magnetism of success, and you will go forth upon the highways and by-ways of life, endowed with a kingly confidence in your ability to win a measure of success achieved by few.

But remember—(should discouragement seek to dog your steps)— every great structure requires the process of time. "The giant trees of California were once puny saplings. The slow lapse of time has drawn nature into their mighty hearts." Just as surely as the absorption of natural forces built the giant redwoods, just as surely can you draw upon nature for GIANT POWERS.

The Fire.

In ancient myth, Prometheus
Filched fire from the altars of the gods
To warm the world,
Incurring Jove's dread wrath
And endless torment.

Lo, mind,—inflamed by the vision:
Of victim and the torturing bird,
Of black vindictiveness and suffering Will,
Rived forever, yet for aye supreme,—
Heroizes the deed and soul
And wreaks on canvas and in drama high
Its passionate admiration.

Now, too, in palace and hut confronted,
In battleship and iron steed defying space,
In flaring furnace of the smelted ore,

In haunts of coal and steam below the whirling wheels,
Life laughs and sings and thunders
An oratorio merging all the powers of harmony,
And hails the high-born Thief,
As giver of ethereal fire.

The atomic thrill waits also the clear call
To lift dull bodies till the joy of flesh
Becomes a common luxury;—
To vibrate rhythmically swift
Through all the responsive cells of thought
Till a man might solemnly hold
All things are possible on the bursting earth;—
To energize the mystic self
With consciousness of life deific
Till the whole world, jubilant, should flame
With its glory, actual, concrete, the one sure Truth
Of a rock-girt globe, or a sun-filled space.
—THE AUTHOR.

THE TWENTY-SEVENTH LESSON—The Four Pyramids.

> This equation's writ
> In every scene:
> The end shall fit—
> As extremes to mean—
> Whatever's forerunner to it.
> —THE AUTHOR.

PRINCIPLE—The best use of self demands that it be understood.

Our ideal specimen of human nature is the whole man at his best.

The etheric life demands (a) the vibrations native to the body in health—(Physical Magnetism)—(b) the vibrations induced by the active mind, (c) the vibrations intensified by controlled emotional states, (d) the regulative vibrations of psychic righteousness or honor—(Psychic Magnetism). In this scheme nothing is inferior, but all elements are appointed to be subordinate to the last. These vibrations should run through the whole etheric activity a binding thread of force.

We are now to study the four pyramids of the etheric life. The purpose is four-fold. If you will put yourself into this lesson as you have, presumably, put yourself into the preceding twenty-six lessons, you will discover—

Firstly—Magnetic CONCENTRATION;

Secondly—The RELATION of the DIVISIONS of self to the WHOLE self;

Thirdly—A better UNDERSTANDING of your personality;

Fourthly—The supreme importance of PSYCHIC RIGHTEOUSNESS.

It is altogether probable that the majority of people live almost wholly in the physical pyramids of existence.

Properly speaking, the illustration on page 422 is a single pyramid rather than four pyramids. It is composed of four triangular walls, each of which is called a pyramid for convenience and represents a certain phase of your nature. The great pyramidal I AM is complete only as all sides of your selfhood are fully built up. You are LOOKING DOWN from the "I AM."

A CURIOUS ILLUSTRATION.

A point has neither length, breadth, nor thickness. Move it in thought any distance in one direction, and you have the line. Move the line FROM its direction any distance, you have the surface. Move the surface OUT of its plane any distance, you have the solid. Thus you have obtained length, breadth, thickness, line, surface, solid, motion, space, time, number, structure, body, and, in the attention, mind,—and scores of other factors (study out a long list),—by means of that which has no length, no breadth, no thickness.

The real YOU is that point. YOU move and describe a line of life. This line, repeated, becomes habit, which moved through time, makes conduct, and right conduct, projected through life, yields magnetism.

If you live only on surface I, you are mere animal. If you
project, that surface through to III, you are a fine moral person.
If you project surface II through to surface IV, you are magnetic.
If you combine these solids, YOU are the Ideal Pyramid, "*I* AM
POWER."

Let us add the following:

"Culture is not measured by the greatness of the field which is covered by our knowledge, but by the nicety with which we can perceive relations in that field, whether great or small."

This book desires that you become acquainted with the unused portions of your nature.

In order to this, you are now invited to make a long regime of mining out the magnetic significance of—

THE FOUR PYRAMIDS.

I

Harmony—
Exercise—Recreation
—Air—Sleep—Water
—Food—Regularity—Digestion
—Cleanliness—Economy—
Scientific Body-Building and Using.
I. Pyramid of Physical Health

II

Will—Muscular
Development
—Nervous Condition
—Inner Energy—
Responsiveness—Self Control—Staying
Power—Health—Body-Tone—
Personal Qualities—Physical Characteristics.
II. Pyramid of Physical Magnetism.

III

Peace—Will
—Righteousness—
Love—Knowledge
Faith—Hope—Courage—
Body-Health—Right Heredity—
Right Environment—Right Training.
III. Pyramid of Moral Health.

IV

Will—Alertness
—Fidelity—
Hope—Courage—
Confidence—Honor—Thought—
Faith in System—Physical
Basis: Health—Body-Magnetism.
IV. Pyramid of Personal Magnetism.

You are now invited to write out all the possible TRUE combinations of these four pyramids, and particularly to observe the following

RIGHT PYRAMIDAL COMBINATIONS.

We see that—

1. Physical Health makes for Physical Magnetism;

2. Physical Magnetism bases Psychic Magnetism;

3. Physical Health neighbors Moral Health;

4. Moral Health conduces to Physical Magnetism;

5. Moral Health is indispensable to Psychic Magnetism;

6. Psychic health bases Physical Magnetism.

We also observe that—

7. Physical Magnetism assists Physical Health;

8. Psychic Magnetism assists Physical Health;

9. Moral Health assists Physical Health.

It now appears that—

10. Physical Magnetism is indifferent to TRUE Moral Health;

11. Psychic Magnetism assists Moral Health;

12. Psychic Magnetism assists Physical Magnetism.

We therefore conclude that the following are

INCOMPLETE PYRAMIDAL COMBINATIONS.

1. Physical Health—[Physical Magnetism + Psychic Magnetism + Moral Health].

2. Physical Health + Physical Magnetism—[Psychic Magnetism + Moral Health].

3. Physical Health + Physical Magnetism + Psychic Magnetism— [Moral Health].

4. Physical Magnetism—[Psychic Magnetism + Moral Health].

5. Physical Magnetism + Psychic Magnetism—[Moral Health]. Impossible.

6. Psychic Magnetism—[Physical Health + Physical Magnetism].

7. Psychic Magnetism + Physical Health—[Physical Magnetism + Moral Health]. Impossible in part.

8. Moral Health—[Physical Health + Physical Magnetism].

9. Moral Health + Physical Health—[Physical Magnetism + Psychic Magnetism]. Impossible in part.

You may thus possess physical health without physical magnetism. But if you seek physical magnetism, you must go by the way of physical health.

You may possess moral health without full psychic magnetism, but if you seek the highest form of psychic magnetism, you must go by the way of moral health.

It is now evident that the following are

IDEAL COMBINATIONS.

FIRST—FROM THE STANDPOINT OF MORALS.

1. First:—Moral Health. Next:

2. Moral Health + Psychic Magnetism + Physical Magnetism + Physical Health. Next:

3. Moral Health + Psychic Magnetism + Physical Magnetism. Next:

4. Moral Health + Psychic Magnetism + Physical Health. Next:

5. Moral Health + Psychic Magnetism. Next:

6. Moral Health + Physical Magnetism. Next:

7. Moral Health + Physical Health. Next:

8. Psychic Magnetism. Impossible alone.

9. Physical Magnetism. Impossible alone.

10. Physical Health. Mere animal life.

SECOND—FROM THE STANDPOINT OF MAGNETISM.

1. First:—Psychic Magnetism. Next:

2. Psychic Magnetism + Moral Health + Physical Magnetism + Physical Health. Next:

3. Psychic Magnetism + Moral Health + Physical Magnetism. Next:

4. Psychic Magnetism + Moral Health + Physical Health. Next:

5. Psychic Magnetism + Moral Health. Next:

6. Psychic Magnetism + Physical Magnetism. Next:

7. Psychic Magnetism + Physical Health. Next:

8. Moral Health. Next:

9. Physical Magnetism. Impossible alone. Next:

10. Physical Health. Valueless alone.

CONCLUSIONS.

Summarizing possible conclusions, we have the following:

1. Physical health is indispensable to physical magnetism;

2. Psychic righteousness (health) is indispensable to psychic magnetism;

3. Psychic magnetism is indispensable to best physical magnetism;

4. Physical magnetism is not wholly indispensable to psychic magnetism.

5. PERFECT PSYCHIC MAGNETISM INVOLVES HEALTH, PHYSICAL MAGNETISM AND PSYCHIC RIGHTEOUSNESS.

The ALL-IMPORTANT departments of your personality are those of PSYCHIC RIGHTEOUSNESS and PSYCHIC MAGNETISM.

But the IDEAL MAN of success is the WHOLE MAN always AT HIS BEST.

The whole man is more than psychic development; he is a PRODUCT AND A CREATOR OF PRACTICAL AFFAIRS.

MAGNETISM A GROWTH.

Let us understand. You cannot reasonably hope to succeed by merely DREAMING about success.

You surely cannot achieve success if you PLUNGE BLINDLY through your career.

You cannot really succeed without possessing some degree of PERSONAL MAGNETISM.

When you began the present study, you certainly possessed a measure of magnetic capacity, either physical or psychic, otherwise you would not have purchased this book. If you have energetically observed its directions, you have developed both varieties; but, above that, you have also combined them into one living whole, the magnetic personality.

This result has required at least a year of persistent effort. If you have arrived at this point in less time, you should go back and begin where haste first retarded your progress.

MAGNETISM IS A NATURAL GROWTH.

No matter how great may be your ability to read and understand books, that growth, that law, require time as well as intelligent effort. No matter how poor may be your ability in such respect, that growth is absolutely certain if you put reasonable time and genuine effort into its acquisition.

The giant trees of California were once puny saplings. The slow lapse of time has drawn nature into their mighty hearts. Magnetism can no more be acquired by the mere reading of a book, or by hurried practice of its directions, than can these giants of the West be produced in the hot-house culture of a northern summer.

MAGNETIC GROWTH IS NATURALLY SLOW. Its principles, its methods, and the results of its study, have to be deeply sunk into and absorbed and assimilated by the subjective self before the reaction of magnetism in the objective life can obtain. This book has promised no miracle. If you have read it correctly, you have learned that magnetic growth cannot be hurried. These statements are placed here because, had they appeared at the beginning of our work, the outlook would have seemed, perhaps, discouraging, but more especially because they would not have been understood. You now understand them because you have toiled, and you can afford to smile at such possible discouragement. You have paid an easy price for magnetic power, for the gains discount the pains.

MAGNETISM AND PRACTICAL LIFE.

The faithful observance of the suggestions of this volume has developed many surprises during the time occupied. It is possible that the lessons have unduly cultivated your subjective life. In a work of this kind, such a danger is unavoidable. The growth of magnetism involves intense and continuous concentration of thought upon the psychic field, and it is very likely that you may find it necessary to guard against that danger. The method of so guarding is briefly indicated below.

The sole value of magnetism consists in its practical application to everyday affairs. Success-Magnetism is not an accomplishment merely; it is a practical power. When rightly developed and used, it controls the subjective self in the concrete work of the objective. The definition of the goal you have been seeking now appears:

SUCCESS-MAGNETISM IS PERSONAL MAGNETISM INTELLIGENTLY MULTIPLIED INTO ACTUAL LIFE.

The first duty of man is practical sanity.

AVOID MERE OCCULTISM.

It is possible that you have now discovered in yourself certain occult talents, such as telepathy, hypnotism, mediumship, clairaudience, clairvoyance, psychometry, psychic healing, and the like.

It would be evidence of ignorance to call in question these "faculties" of the human ego. The author's personal experience forbids. Nevertheless, it is now freely stated:

NO SO-CALLED OCCULT SCIENCE FORMS ANY INTEGRAL PART OF PERSONAL MAGNETISM.

Hypnotism and magnetism are widely separated.

Psychic healing occupies another field.

Clairaudience and clairvoyance are not utilizable by magnetism.

Telepathy and psychometry are related to its etheric explanation alone.

Mediumship is totally independent of it.

In other words, personal magnetism in operation requires NONE of these talents, except, perhaps, telepathy and genuine palmistry— the study of hands as indicative physiologically (not occultly) of present character (not past or future events).

It is a noble characteristic of personal magnetism that, while issuing in and from the subconscious self, its real instruments are the everyday body, the everyday mind, the everyday self, as its real field is the everyday, objective world, big with opportunity, adequate to the splendid development of any human being.

YOU ARE NOW URGED TO PERMIT NO OCCULT STUDY OR TALENT TO INTERRUPT OR BEFOG YOUR PRACTICAL LIFE. All things are his who steadfastly remembers that "life is real, life is earnest." Magnetism is sanity at work. It is unalterably opposed to runaway fads, chimerical visions, unstrung nerves, mental aberration, psychic gourmandism. Magnetism is practical cooperation with level-headed people who are bent on making the best of self and the world through created opportunity.

For these reasons, you cannot study magnetism too deeply nor practise it too faithfully. Its legitimate culture will harm none, will benefit all.

To him who possesses any occult power and uses it nobly, this book extends congratulations.

How May Contentment Dull My Zeal

If one small fact my mind could know
  Of matter or of spirit,—
Within, without, above, below,
  And never neighbor near it,—
This tiny thing a Universe would be,
Clear as Arabian caves to Sesame.

Then should I scan the littlest laws
  Their mightier kin unfolding,

Detect the essence of all Cause
And see the Cosmos molding;
Then should I run, a new-born god, the race
Begun with thought, complete in planet-space.

How might one stay the perfect quest
In surfeit of succeeding?
This were a weak and venal rest—
Vast yonder-wealth unheeding.
This were to make of Knowing that high goal
Which truth declares is Culturing a Soul.

How may contentment dull my zeal,
With range on range uprising,
While growing power to know and feel
Adds to the soul's sure prizing?
Let me, one god, like Him, the Infinite All,
In each achievement hear the Higher Call.

—THE AUTHOR

THE TWENTY-EIGHTH LESSON—Higher Magnetic Laws.

Relays of races, rugged and long,
Up the peaks rising and blending!
Wine for the daring, meat for the strong,
Power with toil contending!
"Higher! Yet higher!" the man's full song—
"Never a last ascending!"

—THE AUTHOR.

Scattered here and there through the preceding pages, various laws of magnetism have appeared. We now proceed to formulate certain other laws that have been involved in our discussion, but not, for the most part, expressed as such. These laws are of an advanced order, and should be exhaustively studied in the interest of the highest magnetic intelligence and power. Necessarily this work must be purely individual and cannot be specifically directed. We begin with

I. LAWS OF MAGNETIC DEVELOPMENT.

FIRST LAW: DISCOVERY OF ENDOWMENT. The limits of magnetic endowment latent in every normal person emerge only through prolonged effort in the culture of magnetism.

SECOND LAW: DIFFICULT ENVIRONMENT. Magnetism develops in direct proportion to the difficulty of environment.

THIRD LAW: MAGNETIC INTENTION. Magnetism evolves solely through multiplication of endowment into environment by the persistent magnetic intention.

FOURTH LAW: FREE ADJUSTMENT. The culture of magnetism imperatively demands that central adjustment of the self to all powers which realizes in absolute psychic freedom.

FIFTH LAW: CONCENTRATION. The magnetic multiplication of endowment into environment is only possible to intense, persistent and unified concentration to the methods of Success-Magnetism.

SIXTH LAW: PURPOSE-IDEALS. Growth of noblest magnetism depends, in the larger sense, upon general adherence to a single, preeminent, ideal life-purpose, and, in the particular sense, upon specialization of the individual in studied magnetic conduct related to that end.

SEVENTH LAW: RECEPTIVITY. The highest magnetism realizes through magnetic laws in proportion as the inner self maintains alert receptivity to the Universal Forces.

EIGHTH LAW: DEMAND. The silent, persistent demand of the self upon the Universal Magnetism makes it a center toward which the Forces naturally gravitate.

NINTH LAW: AFFIRMATION. Continuous, intense affirmation of actual possessed magnetic power stimulates the success-elements, maintains receptivity, emphasizes demand, harmonizes and intensifies inner etheric vibrations, and induces a positive movement of the universal ether and its forces inward toward the central self.

TENTH LAW: PSYCHIC ENERGY. All personal magnetism involves psychic energy developed and directed by magnetic intention.

ELEVENTH LAW: SELF-CONTROL. Magnetic energy concentrates through psychic control of its tendencies.

TWELFTH LAW: MAGNETIC QUALITY. The inner psychic attitude—the character of magnetic intention—determines the quality and effectiveness of the effort to multiply endowment into environment, and, therefore, the kind and degree of magnetism attained.

THIRTEENTH LAW: SELF-VALUATION. Other things being equal, magnetism unfolds as gratifying, but unostentatious, self- valuation develops.

FOURTEENTH LAW: USE OF SELF. Under conformity to other magnetic laws, the highest magnetism issues only from the constant best use of self at its best to the best advantage.

FIFTEENTH LAW: MAGNETIC HEROISM. Self-pity, complaint, and all kindred states, confuse, weaken and waste every variety of magnetic power, while heroic acceptance of conditions for their betterment, and courageous assertion of self as master, conserve and enormously develop the noblest magnetism in proportion to the sway of the magnetic intention.

SIXTEENTH LAW: ACTION AND REACTION. Highest magnetism involves not only studied cultivation, but, as well, the magnetic utilization of stimulating reactions induced by intelligent employment.

SEVENTEENTH LAW: RECOVERY. Whoever, on occasion of any psychic (magnetic) failure or defeat, dedicates the whole of aroused desperation to recovery of ground, infallibly induces a stress in the etheric life around him which ultimately draws to his aid, with the onsweep of worlds, the Universal Forces.

EIGHTEENTH LAW: REPRODUCTION. "Everything is transmitted, everything is transformed, everything is reproduced" (Ochorowicz); in physical and psychic health alone, therefore, are the Universal Forces transmitted through perfect etheric vibrations, transformed through effective etheric conduction, and reproduced in magnetism by adequate and harmonious psychic control of etheric capabilities.

NINETEENTH LAW: SUPERIORITY OF CULTURE. The crude values of natural magnetism, the automatic functions of unconscious magnetism, demonstrate at their best solely as they climax in full conscious magnetic culture.

II. LAWS OF MAGNETIC ACTION.

FIRST LAW: Relation of Power to "Tone." The effectiveness of magnetism in action depends upon harmony of "tone" between its possessor and any other person, and in securing such "tone"- harmony, on any magnetic plane, in any particular psychic state, at any given time, psychic and physical magnetism mutually cooperate.

SECOND LAW: Magnetic Intention. The magnetic intention ("I INTEND MAGNETICALLY") intensifies otherwise unconscious magnetism, and runs through all the mass of general etheric vibrations like a theme in complicated music, imparting to them unity, character, intelligence, and definite and enormous effectiveness in practical employment.

THIRD LAW: Influence of Purpose. In the employment of magnetism, long-run purpose establishes etheric character, and specialized purpose confirms that character if it concentrates the general purpose, but confuses that character, perhaps destroys it, if it antagonizes the general purpose.

FOURTH LAW: Force of the Ideal. Idealism of motive determines the character of etheric vibrations, and idealism of magnetic activities determines the quality of magnetism achieved.

FIFTH LAW: Sway of Other-Interest. The general sway of other- interest in life, and the particular influence of other-interest on special occasions, impart to uses of magnetism enormous effectiveness, and not least in relation to self.

SIXTH LAW: Reaction of Admiration. The consciousness of admiration for others, recognized by them, reacts with tremendous power to stimulate magnetic action.

SEVENTH LAW: Measure of the Intake. In the magnetic life, intake of power is correctly measured by output of power: inversely in waste, directly in intelligent expenditure.

EIGHTH LAW: Adjustment. Magnetic effectiveness is proportioned to accuracy and fulness of adjustment,—to things, to laws, to forces, to times, to situations, to qualities, to facts, to truths, to persons,—and only studied experience can discover and establish such adjustment.

The problems of adjustment to persons are these:

With inferiors, to put self magnetically, without appearance of condescension, on their levels for the end in view,—applying then the general principles of magnetism.

With EQUALS, to apply the general principles.

With SUPERIORS, to assume their level while magnetically deferring, without adulation or humility, to such superiority, regardless of its reality or unreality, for the end in view, applying the general principles of magnetism.

NINTH LAW: THE MAGNETISM OF IDENTITY. The magnetic value of adjustment expresses the force and completeness with which the individual can identify himself with another person, suggesting oneness through attitude, gesture, act, eye, tone, language, and telepathic sympathy.

TENTH LAW: THE USE OF REACTIONS. Magnetic skill exhibits in the manner in which beneficial reactions are received and utilized, negative or indifferent reactions are ostensibly ignored, yet constituted stimulation for further persistent magnetic action, and hostile reactions are refused, without ostentation, but with determination (if worth while) to "win out" through better adjustment and increased magnetic endeavor.

ELEVENTH LAW: MAGNETIC ATTACK. Magnetic success demands the direct attack when etheric harmony of "tone" is assured, but the indirect method otherwise; that is, such attack-methods as will secure that harmony.

TWELFTH LAW: THE CONQUEST OF ANTAGONISM Magnetism ostensibly ognores, and refrains from, exciting antagonism; but, when antagonism is evident, rejects it and proceeds on the indirect attack, or openly accepts it and adopts the direct or the indirect method as the one or the other promises speediest and most perfect harmony of "tone."

THIRTEENTH LAW: MORTAL ANTIPATHIES. Success-Magnetism conquers the influence of deep-seated natural antipathies only by avoiding their causes.

FOURTEENTH LAW: RE-ADJUSTMENT. The etheric life is unceasing reaction, and magnetism, therefore, demonstrates itself by squaring with every issue and making of every change and every defeat a new opportunity.

FIFTEENTH LAW: CONTROL OF OUTPUT. It is an important to know when to open the circuit—that is, to cut off the current of magnetic force—as it is to know when to close the circuit—to pour forth magnetic influences.

SIXTEENTH LAW: CONCESSION. Concession becomes magnetic in its timeliness. If premature or belated, it defeats magnetism.

SEVENTEENTH LAW: HARMONIC CONDITIONS. Magnetism enhances through beauty of personal surroundings,—in cleanliness, order, adornment, art, literature, music, and the like.

EIGHTEENTH LAW: SOVEREIGNTY OF WILL. is the director of native and unconscious magnetism and the creator and director of developed magnetism. Power of will is indispensable to magnetic power.

NINETEENTH LAW: ENERGY IN MAGNETIC ACTION. The projection of magnetic influence proportions to inner, conscious intensity of psychic and nervous states. Exploding powder in the gun calls for the man behind the weapon, and the soul within the man, and powerful vibrations within the soul's arena, and magnetic intention within the vibrations, and psychic energy within the intention.

TWENTIETH LAW: SELF-CONTROL. Magnetic power becomes effective precisely as mastery of self, in restraint and in handling, approaches perfection.

TWENTY-FIRST LAW: MAGNETIC HANDLING OF SELF. The attitude of magnetism,—the magnetic intention and psychic pose,—"I STAND POSITIVELY MAGNETIC TOWARD THIS PERSON OR THIS SITUATION,"— constantly maintained, ultimately instructs in all the arts of magnetic self-handling through the law of auto-suggestion, and realizes in practical form its own ideals.

TWENTY-SECOND LAW: THE MAGNETIC MASK. The mask of magnetism achieves effectiveness when it covers personal states and purposes in a manner positively to attract, and in that manner alone.

TWENTY-THIRD LAW: MAGNETIC CONSCIOUSNESS. Intense magnetic consciousness—without thought concerning it—secures, by its uplifting and stimulating influence, the greatest exaltation of personal powers when employed.

TWENTY-FOURTH LAW: MAGNETIC FAITH. A deep and vital faith in the certainty of magnetic success renders all latent and developed magnetism dynamic, if that faith is thrown into action.

TWENTY-FIFTH LAW: THE DEMAND IN USE. In the application of magnetism to any task, intense, persistent demand upon the Universal Forces swings them directly into the effort.

TWENTY-SIXTH LAW: THE AFFIRMATION IN USE. When, in the application of magnetism, one affirms, mentally, intensely, persistently, "*I* AM RECEIVING AND EXERTING POWER," he unconsciously calls to aid all the success-elements and makes himself a center toward which the Universal Forces inevitably gravitate.

TWENTY-SEVENTH LAW: THE MAGNETIC TELESCOPE. The magnetic attitudes, faith, demand and affirmation, constitute a magnetic telescope through which the distant goal of success is magnified and all nearer obstacles, lures and irritating conditions are closed out of view.

TWENTY-EIGHTH LAW: MAGNETIC ACCUMULATIONS. Magnetism, through correct application to life, not only develops in the individual, but accumulates in his environment, and reacts beneficially without direct personal supervision.

TWENTY-NINTH LAW: THE PERSONAL ATMOSPHERE. The personal atmosphere exactly reflects the inner self, and it furnishes a perfect field for magnetic effectiveness only when the self and the body are clean and buoyantly healthy. [Footnote: See the small booklet, "The Personal Atmosphere."]

THIRTIETH LAW: SUBORDINATION OF PHYSICAL MAGNETISM. In the subordination of physical to psychic magnetism, each finds its greatest effectiveness—according to the relative development of both orders.

THIRTY-FIRST LAW: THE FIXED IDEA. Long-continued association with some fixed, great and attractive idea sets into operation certain deep, subconscious operations of the soul, which, for a time unrecognized and unmanifest in life, gradually and surely coordinate all individual powers thereto, induce a working of the whole system in harmony therewith, and finally emerge in the objective life and consciousness as a unified, actual dynamic force. The idea has swung the individual, has transformed him, has harmonized and intensified his faculties and his personal ether, has come to sovereignty in his personal atmosphere, and from there exerts a dynamic force upon other people and life's conditions.

This book has tried to saturate you with the idea of success coordinating with its necessary elements, and has thus endeavored to swing your whole being into mighty belief that large success is also for YOU.

If you have rushed through the lessons, you have failed to give the above great law its full opportunity. If you have abided with the book, patiently, confidently, energetically, taking plenty of time to work over into your practical life its teachings and directions, you have invoked that law, and, soon or late, you will find yourself a new soul and successful, provided you do not nullify the law by dropping out of your career the practical use of the lessons herein given.

You are now invited to assemble with these laws those that have been previously stated, and to make them guiding principles for life.

And you are finally urged to return to the first lesson and to repeat the work, greatly improved, through which you have passed.

If you cannot do this (or choose not to do so), you should at least constitute this book a permanent companion. You will find, as you refer to it from time to time, that many values have escaped you, that new values are constantly appearing, and that the volume is becoming more and more a friend and a guide. The principles and methods herein set forth should not be laid aside, at least permanently, nor forgotten, but should be worked into the very fibre of your being. You will then, and by so much, certainly demonstrate Success-Magnetism.

Many of our most persistent students have declared that this book GROWS ON THEM WITH EVERY READING. In revising its pages the author is more than ever satisfied that the volume is a great inspiration and of incalculable value to those who will make it, as designed, a Companion For Life. You will never uncover its enormous wealth.

MAGNETISM APPLIED.

Having pursued our work to the present point, little need be said on the application of the magnetic power. The culture of magnetism implies all along its address to life. If you have toiled for the goal you have used the results, and experience, the greatest of teachers, has instructed you in the art of employing the etheric talent.

A few suggestions are, nevertheless, now offered as indicators of the larger possible treatment,—remembering that our field is not general success alone, nor pure magnetism alone, but is the condensed subject, Success-Magnetism. You are, therefore, invited to observe the following considerations:

I. GENERAL LIFE-PRINCIPLES:

1. Magnetism entertains no unnecessary thought of evil concerning others.

2. It is altogether superior to low-minded revenge.

3. It never reveals personal embarrassment.

4. It permits no show of irritation.

5. It is incapable of losing temper.

6. It refuses to exhibit hostility.

7. It never admits, never discloses, defeat.

8. The magnetic person never shows indifference toward others.

9. Magnetism conceals the feelings of ridicule and contempt.

10. If you are magnetic, you never indulge in violence.

11. You neither look for slights and insults, nor do you feel them, unless they are persistently thrust upon you.

12. You are invited to resolve upon the increase of your circle of friends, and never to lose an opportunity of winning a well- wisher.

13. This means, of course, that you retain every friend secured, if possible in self-respect—which should not be unduly rigid.

14. The instant recognition of faces and recollection of names is intensely magnetic.

15. Magnetism ignores all caste distinctions, and is friendly toward all.

16. If you would be magnetic in personal relations, you must splendidly believe both in yourself and in other people.

17. The general magnetic attitude is a close compound of the magnetic thought and the success-thought, buoyant in hope and courage and bound together by the magnetic will.

18. In the use of this attitude, every obligation should be regarded as profoundly sacred. The magnetic person cannot be careless in this respect.

19. This book has all along insisted that magnetic success imperatively demands the life of highest honor.

20. Above all, you are again urged to banish from the inner self fear, worry, discouragement, depression, and every such enemy to peace and power. There is in your mind an UPPER LEVEL; LIVE IN THAT. When worry and the like appear, you will find them occupying the lower level and absorbing your attention. You should instantly force consciousness to the higher ground, expelling these enemies and holding up to the better mood. This is the one secret of victory over the king's foes. The author guarantees the remedy in any case that is not fit for the hospital.

21. In the conduct of life, the magnetic person sets before the mind a definite goal, either life-long or particular, and adheres thereto with bulldog pertinacity.

22. And he, therefore, wastes no values, but economizes all.

23. He saves part of his earnings; he carries his money in his pocket-book, not loosely.

24. But he has the wisdom to recreate, to rest the body, to ease the mind, to take needed breathing-spells for magnetic increase.

II. DEALING WITH OTHERS:

Let us finally understand. In applied magnetism, you simply harmonize the etheric states of others with those of yourself, and convey to them through the ethereal medium the purpose of your will. The FIRST condition of success here is agreeableness, the SECOND consists in tact and perseverance, the THIRD is will-power —not brutal will-force, but magnetic power of will.

In all application of magnetism to persons, you are urged to remember that your very first goal, always and preeminently, is an agreeable feeling within their minds. You should never try to induce a person to act your way until you have thoroughly established in him a good feeling toward yourself. This is the prime initial step. When such a condition has been secured, you are then ready for the magnetic assault—and then only.

When you are dealing with other people, endeavoring magnetically to win them to your wish, you should summon the general magnetic feeling within yourself, will them to do as you desire, and at the same time think of them as already consenting and acting. Your inner condition should be perfectly calm, buoyant, hopeful, whatever the external means employed, your mind should be concentrated upon the thing desired, and its accomplishment should be thought of as now secured. The response of the person may be delayed, but this should not discourage you, for some minds do not take suggestions (those of your unspoken will are referred to) quickly, and they do not act instantly upon their own thought. It is invariably best to induce people to believe that they are acting on their personal impulse or judgment; they should be made to feel perfectly free, not at all coerced, and that they are doing their own will rather than yours—simply because they wish so to do.

We may summarize all these suggestions in the words of a distinguished scientific writer:

"Life is not a bully who swaggers out into the open universe, upsetting the laws of energy in all directions, but rather a consummate strategist, who, sitting in his secret chamber over his wires, directs the movements of a great army." This is a good description of magnetism.

III. THE SUCCESS-MAGNETISM ASSUMPTION:

We are now ready for the great assumption-principle of magnetism in applied life:

THINK OF EVERY GOAL AS ALREADY REACHED, OF EVERY UNDERTAKING AS ALREADY ACHIEVED.

TREAT YOURSELF AS A LIVE AND A SURELY SUCCESSFUL PROPOSITION.

So closes this book. The subject before us has been vast and profound. It is unnecessary to confess that the field has by no means been exhausted. At every step of study its immensity is discovered. Even when the general arena of success in life has been closed out of consideration, as in these pages, Success- Magnetism defies any single mind to fathom it or to bound it.

With this feeling, yet with the confident belief that you are more completely furnished for magnetic achievement because you have read, studied, absorbed and practised the teachings now closed, the author bids you all good-speed in life and signs himself,

Yours for real success,

A BROTHER COOPERATIVE.

PART 22

CULTURE OF COURAGE

The route by which we approach the pinnacle of MASTERY OF SELF now takes a new turn. It is neither that of Business and Financial achievement, as we studied in the First Division of the course, nor is it that of Success and Magnetism as was taught in the Second Division. For many students we now come to the real battle- ground where they must wage the fight for supremacy. The final 14 lessons group under the general title, The CULTURE OF COURAGE.

There is an insidious foe to mastery and freedom, which dooms millions to self-imposed bondage. Most people know it has them in its grip; countless others do not know what the hidden power is which holds them from the richer, freer, happier conditions of life.

This foe is FEAR. It assumes numerous disguises. It appears in many phases of our daily lives. It has done more to wreck careers and ruin happiness than all the wars of history. Hordes of earth toilers believe themselves beyond its influence—while all the time it is riding their backs and laughing at them.

One reason for this is the common misunderstanding of what fear really is. Most people think of it only as fearing to meet certain people, or fearing some accident may happen to them or their loved ones. Yet there are fears of the future, fears of one's self, fears of events, fears of natural phenomena, fears of old age, fears of poverty. And there are still more hidden, stunting fears developed by the un-religious teachings of blind, bigoted, crafty Religion.

Therefore our higher advance to MASTERY OF SELF is up the steps of the following 14 lessons, in which the underlying note is the everlasting declaration, "I AM COURAGE! WHATEVER BETIDES, THE TRUE SELF OF ME DEMANDS COURAGE!"

Dr. Haddock will open new views of individual nature, personal fears, avenues of self-unfoldment, which are wholesome and uplifting for you. The following lessons are more than a conquest of fear; they are A GREAT ADVENTURE into the heart of a courageous life philosophy. They tear away bond after bond of habit, thought and action which have smothered your true, inner Self.

Passing the brief "Introductory" matter, you start in lesson one— "The World's New Dawn," laying the foundation for Courage-power. Dr. Haddock first makes it clear why man is steadily becoming more free—why darkening, dreadful, shackling fear is being dispelled from the world. His second lesson analyzes Fear and Reason. The third lesson explains why the healthy "tone" of mind and body is the basis upon which the structure of personal Courage is to be reared.

ANNOUNCEMENT.

"For all may have,
If they dare choose, a glorious life."
—Herbert.

I have received many letters from people who are distressed by their fears. To every such an one let me send this assured message:

You can grow in your soul a perfect courage.

The methods adapted to this ideal are simple, not impossible to any, and will become less and less difficult as you continue to make them more and more a real part of your life.

I do not say, "Be courageous."

I do not say, "Destroy your fears."

Such advice is common enough, but it is altogether barren unless you know how to carry it out. I hope, rather, to present methods which shall be definite and practical, so that you will be able to do the very thing needful. These methods, in the large, I now announce as follows:

FIRST METHOD: THE INSPIRATION OF THE SUBCONSCIOUS MIND. You are invited, always through the reading of this book and during life, to believe, assume and realize—

_I_ AM GROWING IN MY SOUL A PERFECT COURAGE.

SECOND METHOD: THE ELIMINATION OF FEAR. This is the negative phase of our work. Specific instructions will be given having to do with every kind of fear. I shall endeavor to suggest practical help to all readers for each particular difficulty.

THIRD METHOD: THE CULTURE OF SPIRITUAL COURAGE. By the word "spiritual" I mean not merely religious in the ordinary sense, but rather that kind of courage which is just the breath and tone of the White Life manifest in the human life. The WHITE LIFE in you is harmony with the White Life which is The Good, The Beautiful, The True, The All-Health, The Father, The Infinite Soul of this wonderful Universe in which we live. If you come to harmony with the White Life, your fears will vanish because you will then share in the Courage of the Eternal Good.

There are two kinds of courage:

THE COURAGE THAT DARES AND WINS; and

THE COURAGE THAT SMILES AND RECEIVES.

"And shall I with a Giant strive,
And charge a Dragon on the field?"

In these lines we have the first kind of courage. It is good, but there is a type which is vastly superior:

I AM THE COURAGE OF THE SOUL HARMONIC WITH THE PERFECT WHOLE.

These lines indicate the second kind of courage—than which there is no higher. "Herein is love with us made perfect, that we may have boldness."

These are our methods. They are commended to your approval. I shall try to state them plainly, going on from one fear to another, and another, until the long list is disposed of, and always shall I follow details of procedure similar to those set forth in "POWER FOR SUCCESS," the ideal constantly being

EXACTLY WHAT TO DO AND HOW TO DO EXACTLY THAT.

FOREWORD.

"There is no limit to the knowing of the mind that knows."—Indian Upanishads.

I wish to indulge in a little Foreword because in this way may be indicated a warning against contentment with a seemingly very sensible conclusion which will prove, on further thought, to be hasty and incomplete.

Five years ago I wrote in this identical place in our study these words:

"Fear will never go out of this world until pleasure loses value, desire ceases for want of an object, and reason no longer imposes responsibility.

"The best gift of Nature to primitive man, after reason, was fear.

"The imagination is reason's magnifying power.

"Fear observed and obeyed by reason is a friend.

"Fear and reason take care of man.

"Fear and imagination send him into a panic."

To many minds these statements will have the look of sanity.

But there are others who will instantly perceive that they represent thought on a comparatively low plane. I now observe:

The best gift of Life to primeval man, after love, was reason.

The imagination, void of love,—the feeling of harmony with all,— forgets reason and permits fear to enter the soul.

Fear is an ALIEN to our life, and never a friend. The real friend is reason, acting amid harmonic conditions.

When you are threatened by some hostile force or event, reason tries to induce self-protection, but you know no real fear if you are saturated with the feeling of harmony. You may believe it is FEAR that seeks your self-protection. But your REASON can do precisely the same thing without fear. Fear is, then, only an extra, a distressing extra, foisted in front of reason.

You are invited now to live the WHITE LIFE, to cast fear out, and to make real reason its substitute. By so much you will add immeasurably to personal comfort and power.

Love and reason alone can take care of man, so far as his own efforts are concerned. In properly blended proportions these constitute the very life of courage. What conceivable service then, can fear render any man or woman?

If you desire panic and distress, let imagination fill your soul with fears. But if peace, happiness, health and power be your desires, live the WHITE LIFE and hold fast only to reason.

By the reality called reason I do not mean mere cold calculation and hard logic. Such phases of reason are legitimate in their place, if freed from cunning and deceit, but the higher reason is to these as a woman's love—look is to the glitter of ice. The higher reason is not alone intellection, it is also intuition and harmonic assurance—what religious thought calls faith. The higher reason declares self-preservation to be the first law of life, and then, just because this is true, it cares for self and trusts the White Universe to assist. I really do not see what a human soul need actually fear when that soul and the White Universe are bent on the same goal, the soul's welfare.

The Universe is a growing organism. It is forever striving to realize its own best estate. This is the true goal for all individuals. It is saying the same thing if we affirm the goal to be Health—for worlds or man: Body-Health, Mind-Health, Self- Health.

When any form of health is threatened, you say, perhaps, it is FEAR that warns you to self-preservation. But I say it is REASON, and your fear-feeling is unnecessary and hurtful. If you can remember that the White Life or Universe and you have the same desire, your highest welfare, you can banish the fear-element, reserving only the reason-assurance element. All the fears in the world cannot benefit you. Harmony and courage will sublime your whole life.

I have never known a person whose reason has induced self- suffering. Suffer-fear is always a product of diseased imagination. What some may call reason-fear, when they think they are extremely sensible, is simply fear, and nothing but fear, and it is due to imagination, not to reason.

"But," you say, "are there not all sorts of evils in the world, and do they not threaten us, and should we not forefend against them? In this forefending, how can we escape fear?"

These questions show how thoroughly fear is knit into our very lives.

Now this is precisely the point. Fear has no rightful place with any rightful living, because the WHITE LIFE alone is rightful, and in that life reason-assurance only is possible, and, therefore, rightful.

The best way in which to forefend against evil is to deny it and cast out the fiction.

This entire question of evil is at your command. Evil exists because other people admit its existence. If all were to live the WHITE LIFE, each person might rightly declare, "There is no evil." The only real evil is that which can hurt your best self. When anything hurts your best self, it is your self that hurts your self. The only evil in the Universe is some one's act hurting others, but more, hurting self. If to you evil is, then, it is yourself. You can so live the sublime WHITE LIFE of harmony as to be able to say: "So far as I am concerned, evil has gone out of the world. There is no evil to me."

You see, surely now, that you need not fear "evil." I do not know anything more absolutely and sufficiently opposed to the permission of that self-acting which alone, for you, is evil, than reason. Fear has nothing properly to do with the matter. And reason-assurance has to do with it only by living the WHITE LIFE and denying fear and evil altogether.

You are invited to make these heaven-born truths your own.

I AM GROWING IN MY SOUL A PERFECT COURAGE.

PREFATORY MATTERS.

"The New Dawn"
"Fear-Thought and Fear-Feeling"
"The Soul of the Cell"
"A Regime"
"Fear Not Thyself
"Fear Not For Others"
"Fear Not Dumb Things"
"The Massing of a Hundred Faces"
"Fear Not Thy Fellows"
"Life's Relations"
"The Raw Material"
"Youth is Courage"
"Fear Not Events"
"The Rock of Courage"

The Call of Life.

> Now must the man be summoned forth
> To discover himself, his dual reality:
> His world, ten thousand fathoms deep,
> His star-vault, ten thousand spaces high;
> And come to his own like a king.

THE CULTURE OF COURAGE.

THE NEW DAWN.

"The dawn of a New Day!"
Never an Aryan felt the flare of this electric Fact,
Nor any, or priest at his worship or earth-toiler swarming the land,
Till Zarathustra discovered Ahura Mazda,
Till Buddha discovered himself, the Thou of THAT, BRAHMA,
Till the CHRIST-MIND assumed IT to be the *I* AM THAT *I* AM.
(The flare—the ghostly breath of the long-coming Dawn—
Had passed o'er the Nature-Face, had kissed the swart Human,
Ages and ages, with never a conscious start
In the Man-Soul, till these had upsprung as if gods.—
For, whosoever kens the flare, kens THAT and knows the ONE ONLY WHO IS).
So, thrice have men ventured the Word:
"Comes now a full Day that is New!"
Since these giant Men-Types, what times of the Small
Have opened and set on poor mouthings of Truth!
What Night for a thousand years twice told!
With Fear, and the fierce Stars, and no Sun in the Void!
Shadows—and Fear—and Death!
A fourth time man whispers: "The Dawn!"
We LIVE! And behold a New Day!"
Does the Flare of its Flood-Tide winds stir YOU?
Does the light of its splendoring Sun thrill YOU?
Does the marvelous Life of it stimulate YOU
To a birth of the self and the kingship of THAT?
YOU live! The New Day is for each:
For the hitherto Common Man, slave,
For the Women, no longer a Thing,
For the Child, now escaped from the animal lair.
Dawn's here!
(With Opportunity leading "captivity captive,"
(And the stars urging on to achievement,
(And the Sun, breeding life triumphant);
With heart courageous and faith almighty
To fare forth and possess the whole world!
Soul of YOU, awaken! The New Day is yours.
THE AUTHOR.

THE CULTURE OF COURAGE.

CHAPTER I.

THE WORLD'S NEW DAWN.

"Let us not look at ourselves but onwards, and take strength from the leaf and the signs of the field. He is indeed despicable who cannot look onwards to the ideal life of man. Not to do so is to deny our birthright of mind."—Thomas Coke Watkins.

I am often asked, "Do you think the world is really becoming better?"

My inmost self—the self I trust and try to assist—is sure that the world is growing better, whatever the hampered intellect may from time to time aver.

For one thing, I FEEL that the world's mind is slowly yet swiftly changing its adjustment to one supreme reality—Truth.

Always have men believed that they desired only the truth, and always have they sought and found it in part. But then they have immediately wrapped it in packages and stowed it in boxes with elaborate labels. Our nature craves reality, not wrappings and tables of contents. Therefore every age has torn off some of the ancient outer things, and insisted at last on truth alone. More than during all the centuries before, men today demand reality— just the essential reality a human soul craves, and can recognize, and can use in the building of its life.

Henry Drummond spoke of the adjustment which a great telescope needs for photographing the stars. Let us think of one fixed star. "No adjustment is ever required on behalf of the star. That is one great fixed point in this shifting universe. But the WORLD MOVES. And each day, each hour, demands a further motion and adjustment of the soul. A telescope in an observatory follows a star by clock-work, but the clock-work of the soul is the WILL." The world and the man must WILL TO ADJUST TO TRUTH if they would really find and know Truth.

THE WORLD ADJUSTING TO TRUTH.

I hold that the world to-day, more perfectly than ever before, is urging an accurate adjustment of the human soul to truth—that which alone the body demands for health, the mind for development, the deeper self for peace and power.

The old adjustments no longer satisfy. Truth is, indeed, eternal, but our relation must keep pace with it as we swing through the vast heavens of time. The photographs of yesterday do not speak correctly for to-day. We do not deny the stars; we only deny the science that is past.

This adjustment is a huge PRAYER. It is a request for truth, in a sense, but for truth only. And it is an ASSURANCE. It expects the truth. Now, that is the best kind of praying I know—Expectation in Adjustment.

When you plant your seed or properly place your telescope, you have created adjustment, and you expect harvest and picture. EXPECTATION IN ADJUSTMENT IS ASSUMPTION.

The world no longer merely ASKS for truth; it harmonizes with Nature and Life, and so, APPROPRIATES.

The World's New Dawn.

You are invited to make this thought a lifelong affirmation: IN HARMONY *I* APPROPRIATE ALL GOOD.

Such is one of my reasons for believing that the world is growing better. This attitude toward Truth has influenced for the better every legitimate activity of man. The results are seen in Benevolence, Business, Education, Government, Religion. A new day of splendid, unhampered, happy and growing spiritual life is bursting over the earth. Souls are coming free. Hearts are thrilling with courage. In minds has begun the swing and heave of the sea.

I ask you to take the following lines as a symbol of the world's wonderful sense of appropriation that is everywhere evident.

The sea, the pine, the stars, the forest deep,
  Bequeath to me at will their subtle wealth.
Or still days brood, or rough winds round me sweep,
  Mine is the buoyant earth-man's vibrant health:
All things for love of me their vigils keep—
    I am the soul of health, of wealth.

Run, sea, in my heart!
Pine, sing in my heart!
Stars, glow in my heart!
  For ye are mine, and my soul,
Like ye, is a part
  Of the Marvelous Whole.

There's no thing dear to me is not my wealth,
  And none that sees me I would distant keep;
For swift possession is my earth-man's health,
  Or still days brood, or rough winds round me sweep:
  All things for love of me their vigils keep—
    I am the soul of health, of wealth.

You are invited, now, to seize and use the spirit of this attitude of appropriation for your own welfare and power.

COURAGE ABROAD.

And I hold that our life is growing better for the reason that I discover, in all this new adjustment to truth, this expectation and assumption that Good will not withhold itself, and BECAUSE of these things, a new era of courage sweeping the heart of humanity from sea to sea. There is abroad a Universal Breath, manifest of Life. This breath consists of two general activities, that of Denial and that of Affirmation. Courage is a denial of fear and of the reality of fear's cause. But denial is only the beginning; the really vital thing is confidence in self and in the huge friendly Universe in which we live. Kindly remember this. You are not making progress merely because you turn your back on the Night. Progress means that you also turn face to the Sun and walk buoyantly into the Day. Courage is affirmation:

I am the spirit of the soul
Harmonic with the Perfect Whole.

Why, the attitude of healthy denial is everywhere apparent. Permit me to run over some of the things that are coming more and more to be refused acceptance. You will understand that the items are illustrations only. We are denying: The divine right of kings; the littleness and unholiness of fundamental human nature; a God who is a kind of huge carpenter, a Deity who needs to be appeased; a Providence which punishes; the idea that some people are created for toil and service and others for ease and to be served; the notion that we must eschew all drugs or depend only on drugs; the thought which makes disease an entity; the fancy that the illness of some is a divine will; the feeling that wealth should not be craved, or that it exists for a favored few; the creed that "evil" is a necessary existence; the faith that heaven is reserved for the "elect" who "believe" a number of things; the horror of an eternal hell; the heresy that religion, the spiritual, need have anything to do with creeds, rites or ceremonies; the feeling that success is only for the favored ones of earth; and so on, and so on.

These are merely miscellaneous examples of the thousand old-time "truths" which are now more and more denied. Many pages would be required to set forth the ideas and dogmas which are unceasingly and emphatically being rejected, thoughtfully, deliberately, and in a wholesale manner throughout the world of earnest men and women to-day.

But when you deny, it is a great mistake if you do not affirm something better. The breath of courage which is sweeping over the earth, therefore, is splendidly declaring for ten thousand deathless realities to take the place of mistaken beliefs. I have space simply for a few illustrations. Are we not affirming somewhat as follows at the present time?

SIGNS OF THE NEW LIFE.

Deity is neither Jew nor Gentile; He is the Infinite All-Good—the Eternal White Life.

The Infinite and Eternal White Life is evolving a Universe toward the ultimate perfection of absolute harmony.

All HUMAN BEINGS are in fundamental nature divine.

We are here for the purpose of GROWING TO BEST ESTATE.

Every man, woman and child in the world is ENTITLED TO HEALTH, HAPPINESS, POWER.

"EVIL" is derangement in individual life induced by individual and world-thought gone wrong. As such derangement "evil" is real, but this reality is not necessary or essential, and it may be banished totally and forever.

DISEASE is dis-easement of the matter of a body induced by dis- easement of soul in a body. The self creates or builds its own body, and the condition of the self determines the condition of the body. In "Power For Success" I have stated what I believe to be the growing conviction in this regard. "The sound body is a perfect material expression of the Universal Forces playing into its field, and its physical character is determined by the psychic character of its owner." "In a state of health, all physical movements must necessarily cooperate harmoniously with one another and with the Universal Forces."

What we call MIND is a collection of powers organized for use by the self, and these powers are rightly developed only by the good, the true, the beautiful. If the feeling of goodness, or of trueness, or of beauty, is deep within the subconscious phase of the self, mind-life exhibits as mental health. Mental health is a universal right.

The "SPIRIT"—not to refine on philosophy—is the real self which builds body and may unfold mind. The highest state of the individual, therefore, is religious at the top. This is spirituality. But the only conceivable essential to spirituality is a belief in, and an intelligent (truth-using) surrender to, the White Life—conceived in one's own way—for harmony and oneness therewith.

HAPPINESS consists in being consciously harmonized with the true, the good and the beautiful. It is not necessary, however, although it is, of course, better, to know these words. The child vibrates with goodness without understanding the name "goodness." And so on.

POWER IS PERSONALITY RECEIVING ITS OWN IN THE REALMS OF LIFE.

All things exist for all beings.

Such are some of the realities that are being quietly and potently assumed and affirmed to-day throughout the world. Of course the language of assertion will vary with each individual, but this is immaterial. The essences affirmed are beyond cavil. Other illustrations might be given, but they would be mere phases of that one breath of new hope and courage that is stirring in every land, to "spread contagion on mankind," of the "life which really is."

These higher thoughts, however, are of the Dawn only. The full Day is not yet with us. Shadows still there are, and error, disease and pain. Why must these false "realities" remain? Solely because of three things that linger on:

FALSE THOUGHT—SELFISHNESS—FEAR.

And when fear vanishes, replaced by the WHITE LIFE, selfishness will die as impossible, and thought will no longer be false for the reason that only truth will be possessed.

If the whole world, then, would but thrust out fear and receive the spirit of courage, I do not know any "evils" that could endure a century.

And if you who read these pages will but swing up to the WHITE- LIFE harmony-plane, Health, Happiness and Power must be yours as surely as air rushes into a broken vacuum. If you ask, "What are the limits of this truth?" I answer, "I don't know." To speak otherwise would be mere speculation. I affirm the great truth: All things are yours. That YOU, if stricken through and through with dis-harmony, may be ABLE to receive ALL you crave, I may not affirm. Nevertheless, it is permitted to say:" Launch out! Launch out in the New Thought of Life, and receive, as you do so, whatever is rightly your own, as you are increasingly able to do so."

Man has banished many of his fears already. It is not a long run of the centuries since he quaked before the gloom of the forest, the solitude of the hills, the fog of the vast sea, and, creating innumerable gods and devils by that wizard of distortion, the imagination, lodged them in every object of existence under and in the heavens. He has gotten rid of these.

But when we observe the fear of water, the fear of tornadoes, the fear of lightning, the fear of fire, the fear of disease, the fear of accident, the fear of death, the fear of ridicule, the fear of public opinion, the fear of bankruptcy, the fear of self, the fear for self, the fear of others, the fear of failure, the fear of devils, the fear of a vindictive God, the fear of the future, the fear of a hell—Oh, then, we know that the sun of light is not at his meridian height.

We can yet get rid of these also. This is one of the world's tasks. This is your task, if you would make the most of your self and life.

"There is yet very much land to be possessed." No one will possess all of that land in the present stage of existence. Some will be able to claim more than others, but they will err if they assume themselves to be favorites, and the "others" will do worse than err if they complain, "We, alas, are down on our luck." Be assured of one thing: all may be rid of their fears and the whole mass of distress induced by fears. All may acquire dauntless yet serene courage. In that state, if it be of the highest, as it may be, will come to them a peace, a happiness, an influx of buoyancy, a confidence, a sense of well-being, the like of which they have never known.

PRIME DENIALS AND AFFIRMATIONS.

You who now read this page are, thus, invited to begin our study by denying and affirming, as follows:

FIRST—THE DAILY REGIME OF DENIAL:

I deny the existence of error, so far as I am concerned.
I deny disease to be my necessary portion.
I deny the need of any of my fears.
I deny the reality of any cause for fear.
I deny that I am less than a king.
I deny that ignorance is an essential part of my lot.
I deny that poverty is decreed to me.
I deny that I am low-born or of bad blood.
I deny that I am "down on my luck."
I deny by my life that others are my superiors.
I deny that anything can hurt the essential ME.
I deny a vindictive God.
I deny that slavery is religious.
I deny that I am not the friend of the White Life.
I deny that I am mean, low or ignoble in morals.
I deny that my best life depends on creeds.
I deny that the Universe is not for me.
I deny that health is not my rightful claim.
I deny that I am unhappy or depressed.
I deny that I am weak and a nonentity.
I deny that I shall not unfold forever.
I deny all that is opposed to my best welfare.

SECOND—THE DAILY REGIME OF AFFIRMATION.
I affirm truth to be my desire and possession.
I affirm health to be my rightful claim.

I affirm fearlessness of that which I have feared
I affirm cause and reason only for courage.
I affirm that reason is independent of fear.
I affirm my sovereign selfhood.
I affirm that life is my perfect university.
I affirm that I am success.
I affirm that a part of the world's plenty is for me.
I affirm myself the WHITE-LIFE equal of others.
I affirm my real self impregnable to hurt.
I affirm the Infinite Life to be my Friend.
I affirm that spirituality is true freedom.
I affirm myself the friend of the Infinite.
I affirm that mine is the WHITE-LIFE.
I affirm my independence of narrow creeds.
I affirm buoyant happiness as my present possession.
I am power!
I shall live and unfold forever.

It may be that all this is strange thought to you, almost meaningless, perhaps. You are invited, therefore, to remember that thousands of people have felt similarly at first, have then caught a glimpse of the truth here and there, and finally have experienced a wondrous recognition of the New Dawn which has now surely come to the world. It is significant that these are saying, "There is nothing else worth while in the whole earth."

Two men were scraping paint from a house preparatory to putting on. a new coat of color, One of them who had been helped back from mental unbalance, and helped solely by thought, broke a long silence and said: "This is the whole thing." He referred to the dawn of Real Life in himself.

If, now, this chapter has seemed to broach the subject of religion, remember, it does not deal with religion as you perhaps know religion. The only thing valuable in religion is the White Life within the human self. That alone is religion. Call it what you will. And it means just that courage which makes us buoyantly equal to any kind of life that is right. The methods of this book will prove of value to you, whether or no you go into the WHITE- LIFE phase of existence. But they will realize completest value if you will swing at the start clean out into the one greatest thought—"*I* SURRENDER TO, AND *I* RECEIVE, THE INFINITE WHITE LIFE."

It is because I desire every reader to get this perfect start in our study that I have indulged in the rather general outlook on the world's New Dawn. Hereafter our work will be more specific and adressed to the varying conditions of the individual man or woman.

FEAR—THOUGHT AND FEAR—FEELING.

The INTELLECT coldly reflects What Is:
An icy, crystalline lake portraying earth and sky
In shadows beautiful as death—
And void of pulse, or warmth, or music of good life.
This is no Eye with which to view the world!

The SOUL reflects the universe
With ECSTASIES of heat, of hue, of harmony!
Its INNER gaze creating Life in Fact,
So, robing sheer Reality in colors ravishing,
Giving it Voice, forming within it Heart,
And vitalizing All with Feeling—Being's blood.
This is our Eye, viewing the world it builds.

Fear blurs that Eye, while Reason clears:
Pure mind lacks Passion adding values to existence;
(Who loves mere ghost—flowers born of moonlight?)
Pure Feeling lacks in REASON, needing values,
And, lacking so, fills Eye of Soul with fantasies,
With wild distortions of imagination's lust.
(Who loves the fire—hued, smoke blooms of Hell's Land?)
And always Fear feeds Feeling's grotesque growths
Till Soul's Eye on its own creation looks
As on eternal Truth.
Then Truth and Nature, Deity and Man
Evolve dread enmity and horrors multiple,
And Soul flees terror-stricken on to Death.

Oh, I will rule heart's Feeling for good Life,
Given Soul's Mind for this—naught else:
That Reason may re—think the Beautiful and Happiness
And see eternal Truth and Truth-Fact as my lovers—
Veracious Guardian Angels guiding all my way—
Cooperative, like the brain and heart of body,
To lead my soul on Courage (not on Death)
And make me worth the skill
Of the illimitable years—a Mind—Man, whole!
—THE AUTHOR.

CHAPTER II.

FEAR AND REASON.

"In civilized life it has at last become possible for large numbers of people to pass from the cradle to the grave without ever having had a pang of genuine fear. Many of us need an attack of mental disease to teach us the meaning of the word."—William James.

We have all heard the seemingly discriminating remarks that fear is normal and abnormal, and that normal fear is to be regarded as a friend, while abnormal fear should be destroyed as an enemy.

The fact is that no so—called normal fear can be named which has not been clearly absent in some people who have had every cause therefor. If you will run over human history in your mind, or look about yea in the present life, you will find here and there persons who, in situations or before objects which ought, as any fearful soul will insist, to inspire the feeling of at least normal self-protecting fear, are nevertheless wholly without the feeling. They possess every feeling and thought demanded except fear. The idea of self-preservation is as strongly present as with the most abjectly timid or terrified, but fear they do not know. This FEARLESS awareness of fear—suggesting conditions may be due to several causes. It may result from constitutional make-up, or from long—continued training or habituation, or from religious ecstasy, or from a perfectly calm sense of spiritual selfhood which is unhurtable, or from the action of very exalted reason. Whatever the explanation, the fact remains: the very causes which excite fear in most of us, merely appeal, with such people, if at all. to the instinct of self-preservation and to reason, the thought-element of the soul which makes for personal peace and wholeness.

BANISH ALL FEAR.

It is on such considerations that I have come to hold that all real fear-FEELING should and may be banished from our life, and that what we call "normal fear" should be substituted in our language by "instinct" or by "reason," the element of fear being dropped altogether.

"Everyone can testify that the psychical state called fear consists of mental representations of certain painful results" (James). The mental representations may be very faint as such, but the idea of hurt to self is surely present. If, then, it can be profoundly believed that the real self cannot be hurt; if the reason can be brought to consider vividly and believingly all quieting considerations; if the self can be held consciously in the assurance that the White Life surrounds the true self, and is surely within that self, and will suffer "no evil to come nigh," while all the instincts of self—preservation may be perfectly active, fear itself must be removed "as far as the east is from the west."

This splendid conviction I earnestly commend to all readers.

These are the ways, then, in which any occasion for fear may be divided:

As a warning and as a maker of panic. But let us say that the warning should be understood as given to reason, that fear need not appear at all, and that the panic is perfectly useless pain. With these discriminations in mind, we may now go on to a

PRELIMINARY STUDY OF FEAR.

Fear is (a) an impulse, (b) a habit, (c) a disease.

Fear, as it exists in man, is a make-believe of sanity, a creature of the imagination, a state of insanity.

Furthermore, fear is, now of the nerves, now of the mind, now of the moral consciousness.

The division depends upon the point of view. What is commonly called normal fear should give place to REASON, using the word to cover instinct as well as thought. From the correct point of view all fear is an evil so long as entertained.

Whatever its manifestations, wherever its apparent location, fear is a psychic state, of course, reacting upon the individual in several ways: as, in the nerves, in mental moods, in a single impulse, in a chronic habit, in a totally unbalanced condition. The reaction has always a good intention, meaning, in each case, "Take care! Danger!" You will see that this is so if you will look for a moment at three comprehensive kinds of fear—fear of self, fear for self, fear for others. Fear OF self is indirectly fear FOR self—danger. Fear for others signifies foresensed or forepictured distress to self because of anticipated misfortune to others. I often wonder whether, when we fear FOR others, it is distress TO SELF or hurt to THEM that is most emphatically in our thought.

Fear, then, is usually regarded as the soul's danger signal. But the true signal is instinctive and thoughtful reason.

Even instinct and reason, acting as warning, may perform their duty abnormally, or assume abnormal proportions. And then we have the FEELING of fear. The normal warning is induced by actual danger apprehended by mind in a state of balance and self-control. Normal mind is always capable of such warning. There are but two ways in which so-called normal fear, acting in the guise of reason, may be annihilated: by the substitution of reason for fear, and by the assurance of the WHITE LIFE.

Let it be understood, now, that by normal fear is here meant normal reason—real fear being denied place and function altogether. Then we may say that such action of reason is a benefactor to man. It is, with pain and weariness, the philanthropy of the nature of things within us.

One person said: "Tired? No such word in my house!" Now this cannot be a sound and healthy attitude. Weariness, at a certain stage of effort, is a signal to stop work. When one becomes so absorbed in labor as to lose consciousness of the feeling of weariness, he has issued a "hurry call" on death. I do not deny that the soul may cultivate a sublime sense of buoyancy and power; rather do I urge you to seek that beautiful condition; but I hold that when a belief or a hallucination refuses to permit you to hear the warning of nerves and muscles, Nature will work disaster inevitably. Let us stand for the larger liberty which is joyously free to take advantage of everything Nature may offer for true well-being. There is a partial liberty which tries to realize itself by denying various realities as real; there is a higher liberty which really realizes itself by conceding such realities as real and by using or disusing them as occasion may require in the interest of the self at its best. I hold this to be true wisdom: to take advantage of everything which evidently promises good to the self, without regard to this or that theory, and freely to use all things, material or immaterial, reasonable or spiritual. I embrace your science or your method; but I beg to ignore your bondage to philosophy or to consistency. So I say that to normal health the weary-sense is a rational command to replenish exhausted nerves and muscles.

It is not liberty, it is not healthful, to declare, "There is no pain." Pain does exist, whatever you affirm, and your affirmation that it does not is proof that it does exist, for why (and HOW) declare the non-existence of that which actually is non-existent? But if you say, "As a matter of fact I have pain, but I am earnestly striving to ignore it, and to cultivate thought-health so that the cause of pain may be removed," that is sane and beautiful. This is the commendable attitude of the Bible character who cried: "Lord, I believe; help thou mine unbelief." To undertake swamping pain with a cloud of psychological fog—that is to turn anarchist against the good government of Nature. By pain Nature informs the individual that he is somewhere out of order. This warning is normal. The feeling becomes abnormal in the mind when imagination twangs the nerves with reiterated irritation, and Will, confused by the discord and the psychic chaos, cowers and shivers with fear.

I do not say there is no such thing as fear. Fear does exist. But it exists in your life by your permission only, not because it is needful as a warning against "evil."

Fear is induced by unduly magnifying actual danger, or by conjuring up fictitious dangers through excessive and misdirected psychical reactions. This also may be taken as a signal of danger, but it is a falsely-intentioned witness, for it is not needed, is hostile to the individual because it threatens self-control and it absorbs life's forces in useless and destructive work when they ought to be engaged in creating values. Hence we state

THE FIRST GREAT PRINCIPLE OF FEAR-CONQUEST.

Timidity, apprehension, fear, alarm, fright, consternation, terror, panic, desperation, are all false imitations of reason's interpretation of the warning signals of Nature, to be displaced by reason itself, which may then determine whether the occasion be real or unreal, and always to be disregarded and overcome if evidently refering to causes which do not actually exist.

This principle is adduced in the interest of three things: peace, health, power. You are invited to note how vital these interests really are.

The truest peace, of which courage is a sublime bloom, is a growth solely of honorable living and robust self-respect.

Health is of the following realities: body, mind, soul—the deeper self. Health is soundness. A sound human is a triune wholeness. Physical soundness with weak intellect is often the athletic field of superstitions innumerable. Intellectual greed in an unsound body may breed the direst fears of life. A decayed soul is always a House of Fear. The ideal of human existence is—The white life in the sound mind in the vibrantly whole body.

It is because there are so many people who are in some sense sick, that fears abound in every direction. But—it is because so many fears are permitted and actually nursed as boons that so many sick people abound in every direction. If all our fears could be removed absolutely, we should no longer require physicians. This world would be a paradise in every respect. I do not know anything wrong with it that cannot be traced to a fear.

The causes of fear are weak reason, uncontrolled imagination, want of self-control, and ill-health. And the first three items are really phases of the last.

The ability to master and destroy fear depends, it would now seem, upon the following factors of our life:

The General Tone of the Individual; The Soul's Power of Will; The Development and Balance of the Reason.

Reason is demanded to distinguish between right and wrong causes for personal effort in self-protection, and to utterly ignore all wrong causes.

Will-power is demanded to banish fears and to utilize reason's dictates.

But the sway of reason and the force of action are always immensely assisted by a vigorous general tone of the personal life. Now appear, in view of these considerations,

THREE GREAT LAWS.

FIRST LAW: The warnings of reason are based in the nature of things within us, and are universal benefactors.

SECOND LAW: Fear is contrary to the ground-plan of life. It is no primary part of the nature of things; it is an alien in the world- system.

THIRD LAW: The destruction of fear always follows the growth of general courage in the individual. The fear-brood will not depart until the soul has acquired a fixed habit of courage. Whatever establishes that habit, or spirit, secures the service of reason- instinct, and so undermines and finally destroys the power of every variety of fear. These laws formulate a great

PRIMARY INJUNCTION.

Let your soul be saturated, with the sure conviction that fear is an alien in the world-system of life, having no proper place nor legitimate rights therein, and meanwhile resolutely set about the task of cultivating in every possible way the permanent habit- spirit of courageous living.

This book was written for the sole purpose of suggesting definite methods by which such courage-habit may be developed. In order that our practical methods may be understood, it is now necessary to analyze the subject of fear in its general outlines.

It is important to remember that the warnings of reason, sometimes called normal fears, may have actual causes outside the mind and are rightly proportioned thereto and to possible consequences, while real fear is due to causes not based in reality, or, if so based, is permitted to agitate the mind in a way not warranted by possible consequences viewed by a rational, well-balanced life. Our analysis, then, exhibits fear where reason ought to appear, in

A GENERAL ENUMERATION OF FEAR-CAUSES.

Fear of hurt of self by self (fear of self): substitute reason, thus—just estimate; no cause; cause magnified.

Fear of hurt of self by outer things (fear for self): substitute reason, thus—just estimate; no cause; cause magnified.

Fear of threat by things: substitute reason, thus—right cause; no cause; cause magnified.

Threat by others: substitute reason, thus—right cause; no cause; cause magnified.

Threat to others: substitute reason, thus—right cause; no cause; cause magnified.

Threat by events: substitute reason, thus—right cause; no cause; cause magnified.

Threat by the future: substitute reason, thus—right cause; no cause; cause magnified.

You are invited to work out the particulars of this analysis, and to examine them with reference to your self and life. You will make some important discoveries. One of the many questions suggested is this: Is the cause of anticipated possible consequences justly estimated in your thought—is it a right cause—is it really as you suppose? The idea is that you think of any one of your fears and then ask the question in the form just indicated. Thus we may have the following statement of

KINDS OF FEARS.

Fear of Self: timidity, lack of confidence, possible unaccountable states.

Fear for Self: weakness, anticipated failure, imagined disgrace.

Fear of Things: animals, inanimate objects, physical forces.

Fear of Others: human beings, apparitions, devils, Deity.

Fear for Others: children, parents, husband, wife, relatives, friends, strangers.

Fear of Events: present, future, imaginary, possible, probable, contingent.

Fear of the Future: in life; beyond the present life.

Instinct and reason strive to place us in right relations with all these causes. The existence in us of fear shows that we already are, either in mind or in fact, in wrong relations therewith.

The mastery of fear involves the discovery of right relations, mental or concrete, and the placing of self in those right conditions which are determined and provided for by the ground- plan of our nature.

And the first thing thus provided for is health. All treatment for the conquest of our universal enemy must begin with development of individual tone: tone of body, tone of mind, tone of the deeper self.

I am not writing for those who are constitutionally fearless, but I have in mind all who do yield to the feeling of fear. Our ideal, however, is not a mere animal courage, not the courage of insensibility. It is rather the courage of the whole man or woman making for the WHITE LIFE. If you are only partially yourself, you cannot possess the highest courage. Such courage may be yours, infallibly, if you will but resolve for the goal and go on into the great ideals of the harmonic personality. This you can do— anyone can do. And to come thereto is the greatest thing in the world.

You are invited, then, to begin by substituting in your thought the idea of self-preserving reason for any kind of fear (even the so-called normal) as your perpetual guard and guide. Make it a profound conviction of your deepest self that no real harm can come to that self because you have entered the highway of the WHITE LIFE—THE LIFE OF PURITY, REASON, HONOR, GOOD-WILL, AND CONFIDENT ASSURANCE. Swing your life into the unfolding and infolding of the Infinite White Life of Worlds. Courage will become to you the very breath of your lungs.

I send you this sure message: Fear is dead
In all the pure, by reason's wisdom led,
Who wear white honor and evince good-will,
And trust the self to Love's unfailing skill.
I send you this sure message: Courage lives
When man to Courage all assurance gives.

THE SOUL OF THE CELL.

This crystal of Quartz,—the queen of its tribe,
Amethyst, Onyx, Chalcedony, Heliotrope, Agate,—
Some toiler of old Japan, the Artist fantastic,
Has polished to likeness of ice,
Ruining form to reveal it Fleche d'Amour
That the marvelous, delicate, hairlike inclosures
Of crystallizations foreign might please the beholder.
Herein worked the Infinite well,
And, let us say, too, the artisan patient,
To one limit—significant boundary!
HEALTH!

I request you to define it—configure the wonder
Of this dust-common, beneficent Gift.
Who lacks it, he knows quite precisely his want;
Who has it divulges precisely the thing.
Yet never man—scientist, poet, physician—
In words can portray it—the Soul of the Cell,

THAT lurks only in spheres of the Substance of Life;
Fares past the quartz and hides in the throat of the wearer.
Shuns diamond glory for greater of flesh;
Builds higher and higher to balance unstable
In beauty of male and in exquisite female,
And sends through the intricate meshwork of cells—
Sheer matter, kin of this quartz—
Its evidence: light-hue, radiance crimson,
Eye-gleam, pulse-throb, vigor and nerve-thrill
Of just that common, miraculous Gift,
HEALTH of a body wherein dwells soul.

THERE, say I, the Infinite worked well!
Come now to YOU the artisan's skill for this marvel,
Physical man: to refine and ennoble;
To reveal the inclosure of spirit unmarred,
And grow in the mobile, responsive flesh
Mind perfect, held fast in OUR Crystal superb,
The Universe complete.
—THE AUTHOR.

CHAPTER III.

PHYSICAL TONE.

"In the healthy body every cell is polarized in subjection to the Central Will. Perfect health, therefore, is orderly obedience, government and harmony. Every cell is a living entity, whether of vegetable or animal potency, and wherever disease is, there are disunion, error, rebellion and insubordination; and the deeper the seat of the confusion, the more dangerous the malady and the harder to quell it."—J. C. Street.

The thought of the above quotation does not mean that the insubordination is necessarily conscious to the diseased individual, but that it surely obtains within the physical arena of his life. Because it is not the outcome of his deliberate choice, the case is not hopeless in the nature of things, but is open to better conditions. The deeper self which has intended no rebellion against the laws of bodily well-being may now distinctly intend harmony, and so lift the body to a higher plane.

And the last sentence in the quotation does not mean that you are to undertake a vast amount of hard work, assuming that you are not in perfect physical condition. You are, rather, just to begin and go on thinking yourself in a real way as in harmony with the Central Will, which is our White Life, and to hold steadfastly in the deeper self the ideas, Affirmation and Realization of Splendid Personal Tone.

Some of the meanings of these powerful words will be unfolded later, In the meantime, as all things are subject to law, let us observe a number of the general conditions to three-fold health, that of body, mind and the inner self, regarding their totality as the atmosphere, so to speak, in which courage most easily and perfectly thrives.

Fear in man is a result of repeated suggestion, to which low health-tone is a natural invitation. Health is the primary tonic against fear. Perfect physical health is mere strength. Perfect mental health is mere brain sanity. Perfect soul-health is the whole of the man at his best. When the body is buoyant, the mind clear and inspired, the soul harmonic with all existence rightly in the universe, then is the impulse of fear easily mastered and the habit of fear finds no encouragement. There are, indeed, courageous invalids who have not come into the secret of right thought so far as health is concerned, and fearing atheltes and scholars who have neglected the secret of courage, and timorous saints who have failed to possess themselves of the confidence of goodness. Nevertheless, the eternal law is evident that the one great enemy of fear is

The White Life in Harmonic Mind in Buoyant Body.

A person who affirms and realizes these conditions must, in the nature of things, be possessed of perfect health. In the tone of such health courage is inevitable.

That you may come to this ideal, you are invited to observe the following instructions. Health is a trinity, and we may begin our studies with its natural basis:

THE GENERAL TONE OP HEALTH.

The word "tone" means, "sound in relation to volume, quality, duration and pitch," then, "peculiar characteristic sound as of a voice or instrument," then, "characteristic style or tendency, predominating aim or character, tenor, strain, spirit."

Hence, in the sense of health, tone signifies "the state of tension or firmness proper to the tissues of the body; the state in which all the parts and organs have due tension or are well strung; the strength and activity of the organs on which healthy functions depend; that state of the body in which all the normal functions are performed with healthy vigor."

We thus see that health-tone involves the whole personality, physical, mental and moral.

But the truth of the matter hides in a deeper region than that of mere material flesh or organ. Matter is a form of the Universal Ether, so far as science seems to declare, or, at least, matter presupposes the ether in a state of vibration. Your body is a "field" in which etheric vibrations are constantly taking place. All its reality and all its activities involve such vibrations. The brain, regarded as the organ of conscious life, of thought and feeling, and the entire nervous system, involve such vibrations. And as your thought and feeling constitute the foundation of your moral character, the latter also becomes a matter of movements in the ether.

In the case of heat, light, electricity, etc., differing kinds of such vibrations determine the kinds of phenomena. We may say, then, that there is one general kind of ether-movement for matter, and another for thought and feeling, and another for the moral life. Each individual, however, presents variations of these general kinds of vibrations,—a particular variation for his body, and for his mental person, and for his right or wrong self-spirit. We individualize the ether, Or, we are individualized as we use the ether.

The tone of a person's health is determined by the state of the etheric movements characteristic to himself.

If the vibrations underlying the body life are full and harmonious according to their individual character for a person, his organs are all sound and active. He possesses physical tone. If there is a similar fullness and harmony within his mental life, he must exhibit health of mind. If a corresponding condition obtains in the moral personality, the highest health of the deeper self prevails.

These three individualized varieties of ether-movement in man mutually interact and determine one another's character. I know that this law does not always seem to operate. Poor minds and wrong morals are sometimes found in apparently healthy bodies, and great minds and noble spirits in feeble bodies. But the bodies of the one class do NOT represent the finest physical health, involving coarseness, flabbiness, susceptibility to disorder, etc., etc., and are not contradictions of the law. Moreover, the inner life is not always fully expressed by apparent departures from right living: as you may frequently see in some sudden burst of nobility, generosity, tenderness, heroism, in those who possess sound bodies but are outwardly not particularly refined. The rough exterior may hide a splendid germ of true spiritual manhood or womanhood. Could we look deeply into the physical nature, we should always find the law holding good that our three-fold ether-movements do influence and in the long run determine one another for weal or ill. Where the inner self is right yet the physical tone weak or disturbed, we should perceive, if we had the "spirit of discernment," that the better life within has surely influenced and ennobled the essential nature of the body. It should be remembered that two confusing factors prevail where a fine spirit dwells in a diseased body: first, the thought-life of centuries has, so to speak, warped the character of the inherited body and its vibrations to such an extent that they may not, perhaps (I do not know), be altogether reformed within a human lifetime; secondly, the thought-life of the individual, however nearly right in many respects, is wrong in one particular, the belief, feeling, conviction—an inheritance of ages—that disease of the body must necessarily obtain in some cases at least, no matter what the inner life may be. This conviction is a tremendous force for harm. Invalids accept it as true, and try to be reconciled. But it is not true. The belief prevails, and so prevents the real truth from appearing: that PERFECT HEALTH IS THE PRIMARY INTENTION OF THE NATURE OF THINGS FOR ALL. When we can believe this magnificent truth, we shall be able to see that right vibrations underlying the mental and moral personality must tend to reform wrong vibrations underlying the body. So long as the former conviction prevails, that disease is somehow a part of Nature, the better life contends with a double difficulty, the existing physical conditions and the false suggestion that the individual must continue to be ill in the nature of things or as the will of Deity. The false suggestion should be displaced by the affirmation and realization of physical health. Such a reforming suggestion, made effective by mental realization and proper regimes, tends to counteract the existing effects of previous wrong suggestions and positively to change conditions of ill-health, because fullness and harmony of the three kinds of ether-movements are the designed ideals of our lives and the laws of perfect well-being (what other design can we possibly imagine?), and the good suggestion operates to bring about that ideal.

Let us be rid of the notion that anyone is ill because a Divine Being wants him to be ill.

But we must remember that while these principles cannot be otherwise than true, every individual has behind him, at any present moment, two great forces—the past of his ancestors and the past of his own life. Let us be sensible, even while we insist upon truths which are among the most beautiful in the world. The past means much to all of us. Such is law. We cannot get away from law, whatever our theories or religious belief. To me all Nature's laws are of the White Life and untellably beneficent. The idea that law is something hard and disagreeable is itself a false suggestion and a wrong thought. Law is good. The law that life is determined more or less by the past is a fine example of this goodness. If it seems to go against us in some cases, it surely goes for us in assisting a right past to make for a right future. When it seems to work hardship, the fact is the law is trying to face us about for a right time to come. That is the meaning of experience: it is law talking, to us out of our past. The law that our past and that of our ancestors must be reckoned with in all our efforts to reform the etheric vibrations in our personal fields involves the element of time, which element may be greater than we can control in the material life. This element of time is important because there is another law, that great real reforms in the individual require effort continued more or less in order that all laws involved may properly and fully operate. If the person who is a noble self in a weak body could add to his thought-life the sufficiently powerful affirming realization of physical health for himself and live long enough, I certainly believe the suggestion would ultimately prevail. For I do not for a moment accept disease as a necessary part of human life. Is disorder in your machinery a part of the machine? I cannot see how a continuously perfect self, starting with a sound body, could ever come to possess a diseased body. I must believe that the self, growing to the ideal, may bring into harmony a diseased body, provided its health-suggestion is strong enough and sufficient time is afforded for the full working of the law. The law does not, of course, cover such cases as broken bones, because treatment then calls for mechanical operations, which involve laws altogether distinct from those that govern harmony among the functions and organs of the body as underfounded by etheric vibrations within the physical, mental and moral fields.

The limits set to self-healing power we do not know for any individual case. The splendid general law is not overwhelmed, is not contradicted, by such limits, whatever they may be, because the limits are not set by the original intention of the nature of things, but by wrong living and false ideas running through centuries. As we may not know the limits in any case, and as the great law shines ever before us and is equally for all so far as it may be claimed, and not for a favored few of some particular religious or semi-religious belief, it is ours to seize all advantages afforded by the best medical science together with every atom of power in the white life affirming and realizing physical health at its best. You do not know your own limits; therefore lay hold upon the law, the universal, age-long law, for all you can derive from its beneficence. You are not required to turn your back upon any other advantage, but only to swing the law into harmony with that advantage.

Health-tone, then, is really a triune series of full and harmonious ether-movements within the personal field working together for a buoyant right self in a sane and truth-loving mind in a spiritually expressing physical organism. By so much as it is yours, by so much, in the nature of the case, must fear be an alien and courage the breath of your life.

We may now go on to the general consideration of

PHYSICAL TONE.

It would seem almost unnecessary to suggest the ordinary regimes for health of body. Nevertheless, I shall refer to these regimes because, first, their importance cannot be overestimated, and secondly because they involve certain laws of laws in relation to health which are seldom worked out in hygienic instruction.

What may be called the laws of laws of health would seem to be as follows:

1. Scrupulous Cleanliness of the Body, Without and Within, Makes for Royal Health-Tone. The law should be given rational, not slavish, obedience. Your body and your deeper self are in a constant state of interaction. Material uncleanness consented to contaminates that self. Uncleanness of the self also contaminates the body. The white life requires the clean dress of honored flesh. You are invited, therefore, to affirm always and practically,

> This robe I wear of unsoiled flesh
> Keeps mind and spirit ever fresh.

2. Sweet, Sound and Early Sleep Gives the Universal Forces their Perfect Opportunity for Good. During sleep the Universal Thought strives to restore, as our conditions permit, harmony of vibrations between its manifests in matter within the body and its manifests in the non-material self. The degree of harmony is made less in all cases by centuries of wrong living, the effects of which are more or less accumulated by inheritance in every man and woman (right living, however, promising in the future perfect freedom there-from on earth), and by the disturbing power of individual wrong living. In order, then, to secure the best results of sleep, our waking thought should be kept in attune, by all practical as well as by all idealizing

methods, with reality, truth, beauty and goodness. You are invited, for the reason suggested, to live during the day in such a manner that your last fearless thought at night may be,

"Let my soul walk softly in me,
Like a saint in heaven unshod,
For to be alone with Silence
Is to be alone with God."

3. The Utility of Nourishment Issues From Conformity to the Plan of the Universal Forces for Each Individual. For every human body there is a plan on which it is intended to be evolved and maintained. The individual plan is merely a variation of the general plan of our common human nature. That general plan provides for certain foods and kinds of drink, for the manner in which they are to be taken and digested, and for their utilization in building and sustaining the body. This general plan is varied for different persons in the primary intention of the nature of things. Your food and drink, therefore, should depend upon your own peculiar needs. The science of the matter investigates the kinds of nourishment which you in particular require and advises all items furnishing the material elements you demand. But some individual variations, in respect to questions of taste, usefulness and harmfulness, digestibility and adaptation, are undoubtedly results of restrained liberty and wrong thought-life in the past, either of your ancestors or of yourself. That degree of liberty, therefore, which ought to be yours, has perhaps, come to be more or less limited. It is possible for you to secure a desirable enlargement of freedom with regard to food and drink. Of course you have no liberty in the way of natural poisons and beverages which dethrone common sense. Aside from the limits set by Nature, you may acquire the largest measure of personal freedom in the matter if you will determine therefor in the exercise of sound reason. I have had my experience with things not liked and things harmful—apricots, chickens, salmon—-and today I eat all that's eatable by civilized man, and I drink whatever I choose to drink—alcohol tabooed because I want and need all the brains I possess. It is for you to bring yourself more nearly to the original plan for human bodies in this respect, if you will begin with your inner thought-life and proceed more or less in the following manner:

(a). By insisting upon a LARGER FREEDOM, not in the way of demanding one thing or another, but in the way of realizing in your deeper self the idea of power therefor;

(b). By endeavoring constantly to bring your thought-life more and more into HARMONY WITH THE WHITE LIFE IN NATURE;

(c). By affirming that the food and drink of which you partake will surely MAKE FOR HEALTH and buoyancy of the body; not merely stating the proposition, but, while so partaking, believing the truth and assuming it to be true—actual for you;

(d). By manifesting at all times the mood of blended COURAGE, HOPE, CONFIDENCE, HAPPINESS;

4. THE VALUE OF WORK AND PLAY IS THE OUTCOME OF BALANCING REACTIONS OR RESTORATIONS AMONG OUR PERSONAL ACTIVITIES. If we conceive of any individual as a "field" of vibrations in matter and the ether, induced by muscular and nervous action and by feeling and thought, we see at once that there ought to be an ideal "field" in which all such vibrations are in a state of harmony. The state indicated would be a condition of balance. When activities in one direction are over intense and unduly prolonged, all vibrations tend to a strain in that direction. Such strain— all in one direction—is not normal, because it signifies disturbance of balance. If harmony in the "field" is to be restored, the one direction-strain must be released so that all right activities may recur and all vibrations proper to the "field" may again take place. Always the ideal is general harmony throughout the personal field. Now, some of the activities of our life are normally those of work, inducing corresponding vibrations in the individual "field," and some of them are normally those of recreation, which is a true word because it means recreation, that is, action or rest inducing corresponding vibration differing from those of work, running, so to speak, in different directions, and so restoring harmony. Work and recreation are, therefore, equally essential to the normal life. We have, however, built up wrong ideas of each of these important functions, so that most of us distinguish work as essentially different in its basic nature from recreation, and more or less an evil, and distinguish recreation as altogether and in itself a good. Both ideas are surely erroneous. I know that too much work, and work under certain conditions, cannot be regarded as a good in itself. Precisely the same is true of recreation. Neither, then, is to be valued or condemned because of the kind of activities involved or vibrations induced, but always and solely with reference to the state of balance or harmony represented in the field of the personal self. The limit of permitted work should be determined by that question alone; work should always be offset, so to speak, by recreation. The limit of recreation permitted should be determined by the same question. It should always be offset by work. In other words, the value of either work or play consists in change of activities restoring balance in the personal field.

But work and recreation are not essentially different in their true nature. In both cases we have activities and vibrations. In all cases some portion of the body is involved. In all cases some features of the mind are active. Action in either case is called work or recreation according to the idea entertained regarding it. If the idea is that of TASK, the thing is work. If the idea is

RELAXATION, the thing is recreation. I have taken the task-idea into recreation, and soon wearied. I have taken the recreation- idea into work, and have been obliged to call self to account under that law of balance or harmony. A boy, for example, is sawing wood alone: this is work. Neighboring boys join him, and soon invest the whole place with imagination, all busy sawing, splitting,—playing. It is the idea—that is, the real thought, which determines the names we give the two general sets of activities. Nature will check work-vibrations and restore recreation-vibrations, FOR A TIME, until harmony of the field is comparatively restored, if only suggestion use the magic word.

You are now invited to maintain, IN ALL YOUR WORK, THE IDEA OF HARMONY WITH THE UNIVERSAL FORCES OF NATURE, and the inspiration of the idea that your WORK IS GOOD and is building your self to better.

You are invited also to maintain, IN ALL YOUR RECREATION, THE IDEA OF HARMONY WITH THE UNIVERSAL FORCES and the inspiration of the thought that YOUR RECREATION IS GOOD and is building your self to better.

5. PURITY IN THE SEX-LIFE CHARGES THE PERSONAL FIELD WITH THE MAGNETIC POWER OF THE UNIVERSAL FORCES. In this respect the individual should be as a god. The human body is designed for Temple-Presence of the Infinite White Life. Epicurus regarded it as a husk, but Aristotle defined the soul as the "perfect expression of the body," meaning, not that the soul is a product of physiological conditions, but that it is the TRUTH of body, the idea, purpose, in which only do the bodily conditions gain their real meaning. To this great Greek the chief of human virtues was HIGH-MINDEDNESS, a crowning Self-Respect. This attitude of the self toward the house in which it lives recognizes the perfect interaction of self and body, the one being influenced by the other, and so it insists that no injury shall come to the body from the inner sex-life, or from the sex-life to the inner self, but that both shall be maintained in harmony with the absolute whiteness of Eternal Being.

You are invited, then, to maintain purity under the law of liberty, and to adopt this thought as a permanent law: MY PERSONAL DIGNITY STOOPS NOT TO PHYSICAL DEGRADATION.

6. THE LIBERTY OF CONSCIOUS HARMONY WITH THE UNIVERSAL FORCES EMBRACES THE INTELLIGENT USE OF THE SCIENCE OF MEDICINE. The science of medicine is fairly indicated for our present purpose in the following quotation—from Dr. Oliver Wendell Holmes:

"What is the honest truth about the medical art? That by far the largest number of diseases which physicians are called upon to treat will get well at any rate, even in spite of reasonably bad treatment. That of the other fraction, a certain number will certainly die, whatever is done. That there remains a small number of cases where the life of the patient depends on the skill of the physician. That drugs now and then save life; that they often shorten disease and remove symptoms; but that they are second in importance to food, air, temperature, and the other hygienic influences. Throw out opium; throw out wine, and the vapors which produce the miracle of anesthesia, and I firmly believe that if the whole materia medica, as now used, could be sunk to the bottom of the sea, it would be all the better for mankind."

"It is a mistake to suppose that the normal state of health is represented by a straight horizontal line, Independently of the well-known causes which raise or depress the standard of vitality, there seems to be—I think I may venture to say there is—a rhythmic undulation in the flow of the vital force. The 'dynamo' which furnishes the working powers of consciousness and action has its annual, its monthly, its diurnal waves, even its temporary ripples, in the current it furnishes. There are greater and lesser curves in the movement of every day's life,—a series of ascending and descending movements, a periodicity depending on the very nature of the force at work in the living organism."

There is also in our life a periodicity of the deeper self—a curve of the soul's condition, which varies from time to time. When the curve is downward in both the physical and the spiritual case, drugs are of no more value than stones. When the curve is upward in both cases, drugs may be totally gratuitous, and they may actually retard the combined movements. When the health-curve is downward, the psychic curve may follow suit, but it need not necessarily do so. When the psychic curve is downward, the health- curve tends in the same direction. When the health-curve is upward, the psychic curve usually follows. When the psychic curve is upward, we have the best condition for the cure of disease. But Nature always does the curing. The physician never cures any disease; he merely assists Nature.

It is the function of medical science to arrest downward curves by any tried methods, to take advantage of upward curves, and to know what the curves are in any given case. I call my physician because I may want him when I cannot help myself in these important respects. I will have in my hands the greatest number of the best forces when I am subject to abnormal conditions. I believe that is common sense, and I know it is perfectly permissible to the most exalted faith in the Soul of our Universe.

I am ready to concede that in a sublime state of ultimate evolution there is nothing which a drug or a doctor can do except surgery that may not better be accomplished by the power of harmonic WHITE-LIFE THOUGHT claiming health. But in such a future state disease will long since have vanished. Nevertheless, we do now certainly know a great law of mental power over the body. I do not concede any limits, except as above indicated, to the operation of that law if we could get it fully under control. Its scope, even as matters are, is immense. The law is real, and it belongs to no particular age or body of people. It is as long as time and as wide as earth. Any human being may claim the benefit in total disregard of any philosophy or form of religious belief, provided the WHITE LIFE and the health-claim are with him, under the sole limitations imposed by thousands of years of wrong thought-life in ancestry and similar error in personal past decreasing ability to affirm and realize in a way to secure the full benefits of the law. It is for every human being, nevertheless, to strive for the inner harmony, to invoke the law of spiritual mastery over the body, and to put forth all possessed and obtainable power of thought and realization for health, in good cheer, with valiant heart, and inspired by the truth that, whatever betide, nought can really harm the abiding self. "Be not faithless; but believing."

And so I think that our great Nature-Universe bids us hear these words from the Infinite White Life: "Sons and daughters of the All-Good, the power of thought and harmony are surely for you. If you realize your highest liberty and its greatest efficiency as you now are, you will use, not deny, those instrumentalities which are provided in my ministers, Science and Faith. Must you be a slave either to the material or to the immaterial? Can you not employ both for your welfare? May not the king call in whomsoever he will? All things are yours."

Let us not fall into the old-time religious error of assuming that some particular philosophy or faith which we have discovered embraces all truth and value. Let us not label this or that with our little words, and say: "This is law—this only." The law of thought-power in the physical realm is older than any present civilization. The law of harmony as the supreme health-restorer and health-builder is not a law created by the Infinite during the last twenty-five years. I uncover my heart to every soul who is trying for the best things and believes he has found a true way; but I must not believe that this world has been left in stark ignorance of the most fundamental law of our earth-life—that health in its triune wholeness comes of the WHITE LIFE and the realizing claim—to await the birth and word of any man or woman in these times. It is a little too late. Therefore I say to you who may read these pages: "Stand free! Use every means and all methods, material and spiritual (for the material is but a phase of the spiritual), for health and happiness."

7. THE SECRET OF THOUGHT IN RELATION TO HEALTH IS THE CLAIM OF THE WHITE LIFE CONSCIOUSLY PUT FORTH FOR PHYSICAL WELL-BEING. In explanation of this principle, let us try to

obtain certain true conceptions concerning the material and pyschic nature of man.

All existences come to being through the activity of one Infinite and Eternal Reality.

The medium in which all material existences exhibit is the universal ether of science, vibrations in this medium constituting light, heat, electricity, magnetism, etc., etc.

So far as we can think, the ether is a manifest, perhaps a primary manifest, of Infinite and Eternal Reality.

It is coming to be scientific to hold that matter reduces in its last analysis to electricity and is a complex form of vibrations of the ether within the ether. Matter is not merely pervaded by the ether; it is a state of the ether.

Matter, then, is a manifest of Infinite and Eternal Reality.

Life is a phase of the activity of matter. If we think of matter in its grossest form, nearest to us in the process of evolution, life may be regarded as an entity different from that matter. We do somehow feel that matter and life are distinct realities. But if we think of matter as a complex form of etheric vibrations, nothing forbids our saying that life also is a form of vibration of the ether within the ether. With this view in mind, we shall think of matter and life as comparatively simultaneous manifests of the ether, life, however, appearing only when the state of etheric vibrations resulting in matter has reached a stage in which vibrations resulting in life can be possible. We should then say that life is a product of etheric vibrations emerging through those that have resulted in matter; that is, life is a product of material activities. This view cannot justly be called materialism because Life is, then, also a manifest of Infinite and Eternal Reality.

We do not scientifically know any sort of mind that is not exhibited through matter. The human mind always exhibits through a human body. What we call mind is a complex of states of consciousness engaged in various activities. Consciousness involves certain physical activities within us. If nothing were acting within, we should not be conscious. This has always been true. The first dawn of consciousness in Nature involved activities within the organism. If we think of that first faintly conscious existence as a mass of crude matter, then the self and its body will appear to be distinctly separated in reality. But if we think of that body as a manifest of etheric vibrations in which life-vibrations also obtained, there is nothing to forbid our saying that consciousness was equally a product of such vibrations. If so, the psychic factor was a form of vibrations of the ether within the ether—and so, when it appeared, had evolved to higher forms, was consciousness.

Matter is an evolution, and out of it hare evolved life, the psychic factor, consciousness. But consciousness is, then, for the reasons above indicated, a manifest of Infinite and Eternal Reality.

Consciousness is the condition of personality. When the former first appeared, it was a product. Thenceforth, because personality was a psychic factor in consciousness, it became a creator. That is to say, it was capable of enlargement and enrichment, and so, began to unfold its powers, to enrich its own contents by appropriation, and to organize itself in various ways depending upon its nature in each case and the influence of environment. In seeking to realize itself, as it must do in the nature of things, and in adjusting to environment, which was a second necessity of its being, it began to direct the activities of matter comprising its own body, to select matter from without needful for its kind of body, and to build this material up into a kind of body best adapted to its existence, and thus, by its own character, to determine the character of the organism which it inhabited.

All this work seems entirely independent until we remember that ether, matter, life, the psychic factor, are manifests of Infinite and Eternal Reality. But when we so remember, we see that personality consisting of a conscious self and a body is similarly a manifest of that Reality.

This conclusion will appear to identify man and Deity unless we discriminate a little. Every object in Nature is a manifest of Infinite and Eternal Reality, but the latter transcends the former simply because the object is such a manifest, A thing which is a manifest or expression of something superior cannot be identified with the superior something. I am not the words which I write, although they manifest me and could not exist without me. Every object in Nature is precisely what it is as a manifest of Reality. There is scant freedom in the natural world apart from man. Nothing in Nature could be other than it is. Man, on the other hand, is a manifest of Infinite and Eternal Reality in the sense that he has a body, and must have one, and is a personality and must be one (if he is man); but in the man psychic factor has come to consciousness, and consciousness, as we have seen, always reveals itself in SELF-DIRECTION AND SELF-ORGANIZATION ACCORDING TO ITS DEVELOPED POWER TO THINK OF ITSELF AS SELF-CONSCIOUS EXISTENCE. Were it unable to so think of itself, it could not be self-directive in the fullest sense. And were it unable to self- direct its own activities, it could not be conscious in the fullest sense of the word. Our existence manifests Infinite and Eternal Reality, but the power to USE that existence is determined by the fact that we are psychic factors in the highest sense exhibited in the earth, and the use we make thereof is determined by our exercise of the power of self-direction and self- organization. We cannot help being human beings, but what KIND of human beings we are, within the limits of personal endowments, depends solely upon ourselves.

We may see, then, that the psychic factor within us builds the bodies we live in, so that our physical character is largely an expression of our personal character. Ages of wrong thought-life are behind us, yet even so, it is within our power to improve physical character very greatly indeed.

Now, the power of personal right thinking and harmony with the White Life of Infinite and Eternal Reality may be explained in the following way (you will understand, of course, that the outline is designed merely to be suggestive):

ALL MATTER IN THE REALM OF NATURE BEING A MANIFEST OF INFINITE AND ETERNAL REALITY, NATURE AND HER SUBSTANCES ARE PHASES OF ETERNAL THOUGHT. The study of Nature is just the study of that Thought, conducted in various ways and for various purposes. The Thought, in all its existences and relations, is a vast and complex whole, and yet, from the point of view of its highest value to man, a great Word, comparatively simple and open to every earnest and sincere seeker throughout all the ages. If you will ask yourself, What are the main and abiding thoughts which are embodied in Nature? your conclusion, I think, need not be elaborate and confusing. The question, however, must be asked in a receptive and unprejudiced mood, and not merely by the matter-of-fact intellect. "Every inch of earth, of water, of fire, and of air contains the fundamental principles of the universe, and man is the connecting link between dust and Deity, and can bridge the gulf through the illumination of his mind. The most powerful telescope known to man is mind's eye." "He who has cultivated and learned to open his heart to the touch of outward Nature illuminates his inner being by the elevation and refinement of his emotional and imaginative nature. This is the first principle in the objective world of the higher education of mind and soul. The first lesson of Mother Earth is to instruct her children to be softened and sympathetic toward the moods of outward Nature. Thus mankind softens, broadens, and grows, becoming more susceptible to impressions, taking in the glory of the Divine Architect, which is in the world revealed, and the golden gates of the soul are opened."

Seeking with such a spirit, then, the main Thoughts which Nature embodies, I venture to say that Infinite and Eternal Reality has there expressed itself in these great Words:

Reality, Truth, Law,
Beauty, Goodness, Harmony,
Power, Development, Happiness,
Love, Service, LIFE.

These are the Thoughts expressed in Nature which are manifest of the White Life. For such the nature of things always declares, when free to do so. By so much as any object of existence fully realizes itself, by so much are these Thoughts, so far as such realization requires, made concrete if only we have the seeing mind and the feeling heart. With these powers of perception, the seeing mind and the feeling heart, we come to know that all in Nature is good and means good to every man and woman and child in this world. There is no evil in Nature. All so-called evil in Nature is due either to some phase of her existence wrongly used or to some false interpretation in human thinking. Nature is REAL, TRUE, LAW-FULL, BEAUTIFUL, GOOD, HARMONIOUS, FULL OF POWER, A GROWING ORGANISM, A MINISTER OF SERVICE AND WELL-BEING, A LIVING THING, A LITERATURE OF LOVE. If you refer to microbes, poisons, deadly serpents, and the like, I reply that the perfect WHITE LIFE in man, together with the knowledge of science, would teach him to avoid wrong relations and develop within him physical, mental and moral tone (tonus, in the language of the schools). Thus would he be rendered immune from all so-called evils.

If your inner life contains nothing alien to these great Nature- Thoughts, if you see to it that their character is given your personal character, you will secure in the body a degree of the power of harmony which they possess, and your health will infallibly correspond. Do no mistake this sentence. Will you kindly read it—again until you see what it really means? The only limit to your health will be the limit of your ability to realize in yourself the mighty Thoughts which make Nature what she is. I do not mean that splendid results must immediately issue from the course indicated. Patience and time are important factors. I do not mean that a dying man can inevitably realize these Thoughts sufficiently to recover health. There are limits, not to the law, but to one's ability to use the law. In spiritual effort, effort of the inner self to lay hold upon the Universal Forces, you can make your own personal discoveries. I may not say a greater word. Above all, I do not mean that merely thinking the Thoughts will be enough, in any case. The method is one of realization as well as affirmation. But by so much as you become that which the Nature- Thoughts suggest, by so much will your physical and psychic health come to buoyancy, joy and power. You are now invited, then, to adopt the following as the permanent law of your thought-life:

I am, in every function of my body and every activity of my deeper self, entirely GENUINE, representing TRUTH, obeying LAW, loving BEAUTY, striving for GOODNESS, coming to HARMONY, possessed of POWER, GROWING to better things, full of HAPPINESS, eager to SERVE, a LIVING white life, and a Lover of all that is good.

If you will thoughtfully and believingly repeat this law twice a day say, for one hundred days, you will find life unfolding new meanings, fears fading and dying, and courage growing to real greatness.

8. IN THE MYSTERY OF THE SILENCE THE POWER OF REALIZATION BECOMES GREATEST AND MOST EFFECTIVE BECAUSE IN SUCH A STATE THE SELF MAKES ITS HIGH THOUGHTS A CONSCIOUS CLAIM ON ALL GOOD THINGS. The direct utility of the right thought-life is nowhere doubted. By this the psychic factor largely molds the body and influences its functions. Preceding methods or laws have all referred to the truth involved. But the law of direct realization is needed in order to complete the workings of the truth. By direct realization the self consciously claims the present benefit of the spirit or attitude of harmony. You may think of yourself as splendidly well and fearless: that is one thing-you REGARD yourself as in such conditions. And you may claim yourself NOW to be well and courageous: that is another thing—you TREAT yourself for health and fearlessness. When you think of your arm as moving, it does not necessarily move; you have merely entertained the idea. When you will your arm to move, you have claimed your power to move it and have realized the power—realized in actual thought that power. The difference would obtain if your arm were bound: you could still realize in thought the sense of movement. Realization of the Eternal Thoughts is a conscious claim in spirit and appropriation in spirit of the Thoughts as actual within yourself. Realization of benefits for health is a conscious holding of them in mind as present in you. One may in time acquire the fixed mood of realization, but it will assist you to bring about that mood if you will occasionally, say once a day, shut out all disturbances and alien thoughts and feelings, and try to come into communion with the White Life—go into the silence and, by quiet affirmation and sincere, trustful realization, claim the Universal Forces as your helpers in building up your physical tone and the spirit of courage. A sentence like the following may be used:

"Conscious of psychic uprightness in the white life, and of the beauty, utility and wonder of my physical being in its nature, and function, I now claim, and without doubt am receiving, the Universal Forces for my best tone and courage-spirit in all- improving health."

CPSIA information can be obtained
at www.ICGtesting.com
Printed in the USA
LVHW041019020323
740706LV00008B/1088

9 789356 902053